Spring Training

*B*ooks by William Zinsser

Spring
Training

WILLIAM ZINSSER

1817

HARPER & ROW, PUBLISHERS, New York
Cambridge, Grand Rapids, Philadelphia, St. Louis,
San Francisco, London, Singapore, Sydney, Tokyo

Chapter 15 of this book first appeared in *The American Scholar*.

Designer: Cassandra J. Pappas

Library of Congress Cataloging-in-Publication Data

Zinsser, William Knowlton.
  Spring training.

  Bibliography: p.
  Includes index.
    1. Baseball—Training. 2. Pittsburgh Pirates
(Baseball team) I. Title.
  GV875.6.Z56 1989   796.357'64'0974886   88-43003
  ISBN 0-06-016059-4

For my son
John William Zinsser
With love

Contents

Illustrations follow page 152.

CHAPTER *1*

Rites of Spring

This book was born, though I didn't know it at the time, seven years ago in Winter Haven, Florida, at the spring training camp of the Boston Red Sox. I was sitting in the grandstand in a sea of codgers, codging the time away. The sun was warm, the grass was green, and the air was alive with the sounds of rebirth: bat meeting ball, ball meeting glove, players and coaches chattering across the diamond. They were sounds that hadn't been heard in the land since the World Series ended in October.

I was a pilgrim on an old American pilgrimage. Every winter since the early 1920s, families from all over the United States have journeyed to small towns in Florida—and, more recently, the Southwest—to watch their favorite baseball teams get in shape for the season and look over the new crop of rookies. I grew up on the names of those Florida towns. Lakeland! Vero Beach! Clearwater! Bradenton! Of all the romantic datelines in the newspapers of my boyhood—the *New York Herald Tribune,* the *New York Times* and the baseball-obsessed *New York Sun*—

none sent as strong a message as those towns in the "Grapefruit League" that annually came out of hibernation. To every baseball fan stuck in the frozen North they shouted the good news: the long freeze is over.

To be a codger it is only necessary to have a brain crammed with baseball memories, and I had several generations' worth, going back to my boyhood team—the New York Giants of Carl Hubbell, Bill Terry and Mel Ott. Much of my youth was spent—and by no means misspent—in the narrow Polo Grounds, which had absurdly short right-field and left-field foul lines and a vast center field, ending at the clubhouse stairs 475 feet away. Any batter who hit a ball that far could expect it to land for an inside-the-park home run. Vic Wertz of the Cleveland Indians certainly had that expectation, and so did I, and so did every other fan at the first game of the 1954 World Series when Wertz—in the eighth inning, with Larry Doby and Al Rosen on base—drove an immense blast far over the head of the Giants' center fielder. Willie Mays' astonishing catch at the foot of the stairs, which so dispirited the Indians that they lost the Series in four straight games, remains as vivid in my memory as if it happened yesterday. Not long after that the Giants closed the memory bank and moved to San Francisco, leaving me teamless. The Polo Grounds was torn down and replaced by a clump of apartment buildings. To this day, however, I can still see it there by the Harlem River—a longitudinal structure of dark green wood, rickety and amiable. It made me forever partial to ballparks that had a personality of their own and that weren't prisoners of symmetry.

When I later left New York myself and spent a decade in New England, I rooted for the Boston Red Sox. There was no question of giving my heart to the Yankees; as a Giant fan, I hated the Yanks with a fervor that is still coded into my metabolism. One of the pleasures of being a Red Sox fan was the pleasure of watching games in Fenway Park. No other stadium was so human in scale; the players could actually be heard talking to each other. Like many old ballparks, Fenway had been laid out in obedience to existing street patterns and was thus an organic part of its city, forever ordained to have a short left-field wall, the "green monster" that has terrified so many pitchers, just as Bedford Avenue, which ran behind the right-field fence of Ebbets Field, was entwined with the lives of fans listening to Brooklyn Dodgers games on the radio. "There's a long drive to right field, and it's . . . it's . . . in Bedford Avenue!" was the best or worst of sentences.

Reared on such quirky ballparks, I am uneasy with stadiums that are too perfect and too removed from their city. Imperfection is a tonic in baseball—the uninvited guest who never runs out of surprises for the fan who thinks he has seen it all. I'm also uneasy with efforts to improve a game that needs no improving: to hype its rhythm with organ music, to alter its subtle balance with designated hitters, to replace with carpeting the very grass it's played on. At least at the Red Sox spring training camp, I thought, I would find the game preserved in its classic simplicity.

From the moment I got to Winter Haven the omens were right. The Red Sox ballpark had the same relaxed charm as its dowager mother in Boston. Jim Rice was doing stretching exercises along the third-base line, almost near enough to touch. Carl Yastrzemski was talking with two fans at the railing. Johnny Pesky, long retired as a Boston shortstop and now a coach, was playing pepper with Dwight Evans. Other coaches were hitting fungoes eternally into the Florida sky. Winter Haven indeed! Winter Heaven was more like it.

I bought a hot dog and a beer and took a seat in the stands. A rookie left-hander was on the mound, warming up for an intrasquad game. I was enjoying his form, wondering if this would be his year to make it to the big leagues. I told the man next to me that the young pitcher reminded me of Warren Spahn. The man said he thought he looked like Preacher Roe. His wife said the kid was a ringer for Harvey Haddix. An old codger mentioned Lefty Grove. A young codger mentioned Vida Blue. We were typical springtime fools, seeing what we wanted to see.

The game began. Nobody cared who won; that wasn't the point. The point was to train and to teach—to get the club tuned for the long season ahead. Even the veterans looked young. I thought of how often the sportswriter Red Smith reminded us that baseball is a game that little boys play. That truism would never be truer than in spring training. Soon enough the media would age these boys beyond their years by harping on their contracts and their agents, their sulks and their scrapes and their sore arms. But for six weeks in February and March they were allowed to be what they were: young men who played a wonderful game wonderfully well.

Even the Red Sox manager, Ralph Houk, looked human. I saw no sign of the tormented soul that every manager becomes when the season begins, prowling the dugout and popping Rolaids to calm the furies in his stomach. Several codgers around me remembered how tough Houk was when he came up to the Yankees in 1947. Now they called to the "Iron

Major" and asked if he was going to bring Boston a pennant this year. He ambled over to the railing and chatted with them about the team and its chances; he was everybody's next-door neighbor, talking about his lawn and his power tools. Spring training had turned even the Iron Major to some softer metal.

So the afternoon slipped by in contentment. The ancient rhythms and continuities of the game were intact; we could have been watching a game in 1882, not 1982. No organist toyed with our emotions, no electronic scoreboard told us when to cheer. We were suspended in a unique pocket of time, unlike any other season in baseball's long year. It was a time of renewal for both the players and the fans. It was a time for looking both forward and back—forward to the new season and as far back as the oldest codger could recall—and what made it all work was memory. Memory was the glue that held baseball together as the continuing American epic.

*

Last year an editor asked me if I had ever thought of writing a book about baseball. I never had; my baseball writing consisted mainly of brief memoirs. Nor was I sure that baseball needed another book—it was hardly a threatened species. Writing about baseball seemed to be some kind of validating rite for the American male; no game is more deeply connected to the American psyche. Psychiatrists would say that we write about baseball to cling to our youth and to stay plugged into the long stream of collective lore. As therapy, however, it has its risks; the classics of the literature—Ring Lardner's *You Know Me, Al,* Mark Harris's *Bang the Drum*

Slowly, Roger Kahn's *The Boys of Summer*—are tinged with sadness and loss. The reality of baseball is finally no different from anybody else's reality. Even the boys of summer grow old.

Still, I liked the idea of writing a whole book about baseball—combining my vocation and my addiction. But was any subject left? I rummaged in my memory grooves to see what images might turn up. I thought of all the summer evenings of my boyhood when I switched my Philco radio to WOR at seven o'clock—the family dinner had to wait—to get the ball scores from Stan Lomax. Lomax's headlong voice conveyed more information in fifteen minutes than most people could in an hour. I thought of all the candy-and-cigar stores where I tried to track down the few cards that were still missing from my Big League Gum collection. The name of the cigar, in ornate script, formed a stained-glass panel in the store window, calling me on: *Optimo! La Primadora! Garcia Grande!* I remembered the hundreds of hours I spent playing a mechanical game called Baseball, which had a metal prong that delivered three kinds of pitches to a "batter" holding a bat on a tightly coiled spring. My friend Charlie Willis and I once played twenty-two games in one day, keeping complete box scores for our respective teams, the Yankees and the Tigers. I thought of all the games I tried to organize—a Charlie Brown ever hopeful of finding enough players to form two teams—and of all the games I played alone against the side of our house with a tennis ball, impersonating all eighteen players on two major league clubs. If my parents had only looked out the window they could have seen Ted Williams. I thought of my only home run; it came back unannounced and previously unremembered from my World War II army days—a low line drive that skipped past the right fielder and rolled down a hill in Naples, giving me ample time to round the bases. I thought of all the ballparks I had sat in, all the games I had heard on the radio, all the games I had stayed up to watch on TV after everyone else had gone to bed.

But one memory that came back insistently was of the day I spent at the Red Sox camp in Winter Haven. Much of what I loved about the game had been compressed into that afternoon. Had a book ever been written about spring training? I couldn't think of one. I liked the fact that spring training was a time of teaching and learning. That was a process that interested me; I was a teacher myself. I also liked the fact that at a spring training camp the fans and the players could still be part of each other's lives. Historically, baseball is a product of rural and small-town America, and most of the young men on the diamond are the same people as the grown men and women in the stands. Nowhere would that sense of shared values—of baseball as a common American possession—be more palpable than in a Florida spring training town.

I decided to go in search of that once-a-year relationship between a major league team and its wintertime town.

CHAPTER *2*

The Pirates

But which team? And which town? Much as
I had savored my day in Winter Haven, I didn't want to write
about the Red Sox. They were too Eastern, too patrician, too
white. They were also too written-about—a favorite subject of
authors who found some kind of epiphany in rooting for a
team that would always let them down. I never became *that*
much of a Red Sox fan; guilt is no part of what I bring to the
ballpark. Nor do I have any patience with the idea of baseball
as a metaphor. Baseball is baseball.

I wanted a team from the heartland—one that had long been
a fixture of its city and its region. That ruled out all the new
"expansion" clubs and all the franchises that had moved from
one city to another. I also wanted a team that trained in Florida;
that ruled out all the clubs that trained in Arizona. My ideal
choice was the St. Louis Cardinals because they are a Mississippi River club. The Mississippi is one of America's four
central myths, the others being Abraham Lincoln, the Civil
War and baseball, and any writer who can get two myths for

the price of one is ahead before he starts. But the Cardinals train in St. Petersburg and have long shared that city with other major league clubs, most recently the Mets. I wanted no such divided affections.

Detroit was a good possibility. I've always liked the Tigers, and they trained in Lakeland, another small town that comes alive with the annual arrival of its adopted sons. But I was a National League fan; mine was the older and purer league, scornful of such adulterants as the designated hitter. The Phillies? A fine old club, but they trained in Clearwater, and Clearwater wasn't Lakeland or Winter Haven; it was a Gulf Coast town—its heart was at the beach and out on the boat. The Reds? Another great old club, but they had just moved to a new park in a place called Plant City.

Who was left? I went back to my list. The Pirates. They trained in Bradenton. That rang some bells. Bradenton and I went back a long way together. Major league clubs had trained in Bradenton as long as I had been following baseball—since the Cardinals of Dizzy Dean's "Gas House Gang"—and undoubtedly longer. As far as I knew, Bradenton had no other identity, unlike its upscale neighbor, Sarasota, which had museums and other cultural shrines. I called a friend who grew up in Bradenton and asked what he could tell me. He said that the Pirates had trained in Bradenton for twenty years; that the city had an active Pirates Boosters Club; that McKechnie Field, which was downtown, was the most old-timey of all the old-time spring training ballparks; that Dizzy Dean had owned a gas station there during the Cardinals' tenure, and that Edd Roush, the oldest living member of the Baseball Hall of Fame, had been a winter resident since 1952.

"Say no more," I told him. I was especially glad to hear that the ballpark was within the city limits. My hometown New York Mets, after twenty-six years in St. Petersburg, had just built a sophisticated training complex near Port St. Lucie, on Florida's other coast, choosing a site so far from any human settlement that it still had no access roads or lodgings for the press. One local radio station ran a contest offering a prize to anyone who could name five interesting things for the players to do there.

Bradenton looked just right—and so, I suddenly realized, did the Pirates. All kinds of half-forgotten memories tumbled into place. I remembered that Pittsburgh had been my favorite National League team after the Giants when I was growing up. I always tried to get to the Polo Grounds when the Bucs (as they are popularly called) were in town. I can still picture Paul and Lloyd Waner in right field and center field, and the equally heroic Pie Traynor at third base, and the formidable Arky Vaughan, who one year hit .385, at shortstop. Best of all, I can still picture Honus Wagner, rapping out grounders for infield practice. The greatest shortstop of all time, who played his entire career with Pittsburgh, from 1900 to 1917, was then a Pirate coach. Age had made him so bowlegged that I had trouble envisioning him as the greatest shortstop of all time. But I took it on faith. Honus was my link to the gods on Mount Olympus.

Nor did I forsake the team as an adult; Pittsburgh and I have had on-and-off flirtations ever since. I followed Ralph Kiner as he led the league in home runs in all seven of his full seasons with the Pirates (1946–1952). I jumped at a chance to go to Pittsburgh for the opening game of the 1960 World Series, against the Yankees. Baseball fever in Forbes Field that October was as high as I've ever seen it; one fan had the year's rallying cry—BEAT 'EM BUCS!—painted on his bald head. Roberto Clemente, who would give Pittsburgh class for eighteen years, as authentic a god as Honus Wagner had been a half century earlier, was then in his seventh season. The Clemente era ended in a plane crash in 1972, but the team had one more folk hero up its sleeve. When the thirty-nine-year-old Willie Stargell jollied the Pirates to their last pennant, in 1979, completing the myth by getting twelve hits in the World Series and homering in the seventh game to take it all from the Orioles, I was at my TV set, urging them on. Beat 'em, Bucs!

But after that it was sharply downhill—a descent that brought the Pirates to the end of the 1985 season in public disgrace. Sapped by a drug scandal that ended in an ugly trial, stuck with players who were regarded as overindulged, overweight and overpaid, they limped to a won-and-lost record of 57 and 104. Only two Pittsburgh clubs had ever lost more. Abandoned by their fans, who turned increasingly to the city's hard-playing Steelers football team, the Pirates were in such grim financial shape that their longtime owners, the Galbreath family, announced that they would have to move the club somewhere else.

"Say it ain't so!" is a phrase that originated in baseball—it was addressed to "Shoeless Joe" Jackson by a Chicago street urchin when he heard that his hero had helped throw the World Series in the "Black Sox" scandal of 1919. ("Street urchin" is obligatory in telling the story.) The same incredulous cry, if not in those words, was heard in Pittsburgh in 1985 when the Pirates said they would be leaving. They were just two years shy of their one hundredth birthday as a National League club, having made their debut as the Alleghenies on April 30, 1887, in Recreation Park. ("Pud" Galvin scattered ten hits to beat Chicago, 6–2.) In 1909, since renamed the Pirates, they moved to their congenial new ballpark, Forbes Field, remaining there until Three Rivers Stadium was built in 1970. Nowadays the ghost of Forbes Field is cradled in the nostalgic glow of memory by Pirate fans. Of all the glorious moments in its sixty-one-year history, none is recalled with more passion—especially by people who weren't there—than the home run that Bill Mazeroski hit over the left-field wall in the ninth inning of the seventh game of the 1960 World Series to beat the Yankees. Today the University of Pittsburgh graduate schools occupy that hallowed left-field soil, but the actual brick wall, with a plaque to mark the spot where Maz's hit cleared it, still stands, and in nearby Forbes Quadrangle the old ballpark's home plate is preserved under glass. You could look it up.

Forced by the Galbreaths to think the unthinkable, Pittsburgh rallied to the rescue of its team in October of 1985. Nine corporations and four individuals reluctantly paid two million dollars each to buy the Pirates and keep them in Pittsburgh. They promised a housecleaning and a fresh start. Most of the new owners had names synonymous with the city's mighty capitalist past: Alcoa, Westinghouse, the Mellon Bank, Carnegie-Mellon University, PPG (formerly Pittsburgh Plate Glass), USX (formerly U.S. Steel). Pittsburgh's past, however, was mightier than its present—the city was still punchy from the closing of its steel mills and the resulting unemployment that had depressed its economy and its morale. The investors who saved the Pirates had been dragooned, it was felt, into a high-minded act of civic folly.

Nor did their first important decision make them look less foolish: they appointed as general manager a man nobody had heard of, Sydnor W. Thrift, Jr., who had been out of baseball for a decade—in real estate, God forbid!—and whose main experience had been in scouting. The press conference at which Thrift was introduced so dismayed the assembled sportswriters that they laughed openly at his seeming lack of fitness for the job. Two weeks later his own first important decision—the appointment of a new field manager to replace Chuck Tanner—got an equally cool reception. Jim Leyland was as unheard of as Thrift: a forty-year-old minor league manager who had never played or managed in the majors. The idea that these two unknowns might resuscitate an expiring franchise doesn't seem to have been seriously entertained in their new city.

Thrift, true to his name, moved decisively to cut the bloated payroll, rebuild the farm system and the scouting staff, and pin his future on youth. By the middle of his second season he had traded away every Pirate veteran—six million dollars' worth of salaries went with them—and in return he got twenty-four players whose average age was twenty-five. Typical of all this traffic was the departure of three proven older pitchers, Rick Reuschel, Rick Rhoden and Don Robinson, and the arrival of three unproven younger ones, Doug Drabek, Brian Fisher and Jeff Robinson.

One trade in particular outraged the Pittsburgh community. The fact that it was announced on April 1, 1987, struck the press as apt, Thrift obviously being the ultimate April fool. His trade sent the thirty-year-old catcher Tony Peña, one of the team's few genuine stars and a local favorite, to the Cardinals for the platooning right fielder Andy Van Slyke, the little-known catcher Mike LaValliere, and a kid pitcher named Mike Dunne, who was still in the minor leagues. By August, however, it was clear that a heist had been perpetrated under the nose of the Cardinals' Whitey Herzog. Van Slyke, installed in center field, came of age at twenty-six as one of the league's best offensive and defensive outfielders; LaValliere, also twenty-six, hit .300, won the Gold Glove Award, and led all major league catchers in throwing out base-stealers; and Dunne, called up from Vancouver in June, won 13 and lost 6 and was named National League Rookie Pitcher of the Year. (Peña, meanwhile, appears to have peaked.) What was also becoming clear was that people who laughed at Syd Thrift were probably not having the last laugh.

I knew none of this history when I decided to write about the Pirates. Like most baseball fans, I had stopped following the club when it hit skid row. I didn't know a single fact about Syd Thrift or Jim Leyland: what they looked like, where they came from, what kind of men they were. I didn't know who Leyland's coaches were, and I had heard of only three of his players: Andy Van Slyke, whom I had seen on TV during his Cardinal years; pitcher Bob Walk, the club elder at the age of thirty-one, and relief pitcher Jim Gott, who was the senior Pirate in major league experience—six years.

As for the club's performance, I knew that in Leyland's first season, 1986, the Pirates had again finished last—whatever rebuilding was being done wasn't yet visible—and that well into the 1987 season it didn't look much better. But then something happened that caught the eye of even the most somnolent fan: the Pirates won 27 of their last 38 games, finishing in a fourth-place tie with the Phillies. A .710 percentage in baseball is no accident—somebody had been doing some teaching and some motivating. The turnaround had begun.

I liked the idea of so many fresh starts. The city of Pittsburgh had started its own climb back; it would respond to a young team that hustled. I also liked the idea of seeing spring training through the experience of a club that had no stars. As a New Yorker, I had my baseball filtered through the white glare of celebrity. The Yankees and the Mets together had six or seven stars of brightest magnitude, both clubs had managers who were media darlings, and one of them had a principal owner who was a media hog—a summer-long public nuisance. Much of the media coverage of baseball in New York had nothing to do with baseball.

I wanted the game given back to me. If any moment in the calendar could bestow that gift it would be spring training, and if any team could, it might be the Pittsburgh no-names. I was also starting fresh myself. I had never done any sports reporting, never interviewed a professional athlete. I had no inside information; the questions I would ask would be the questions that occurred to me as a fan. I would write out of my writer's curiosity and my lifelong love of the game.

I called the Pirates to get their permission and called an airline to get a ticket to Bradenton.

CHAPTER 3

Florida Days

On September 19, 1913, the president of the St. Louis Browns, Robert L. Hedges, arrived by train at St. Petersburg, Florida, a fishing town of three thousand people, and was met by a deputation from the local board of trade. The Browns had held their 1912 spring training in Montgomery, Alabama, and had finished seventh; this year they had trained in Waco, Texas, and finished last. Perhaps a spring training camp in Florida was what the club needed. It certainly couldn't hurt.

"Hedges was taken to several possible sites," according to Jabbo Gordon, a former sports editor of the *Bradenton Herald*, who described the visit in a talk to the Manatee County Historical Society in 1970, "and he seemed to like them all. He was particularly impressed when his fishing party captured a nine-foot-long, 500-pound shark. A picture with Hedges and his friends standing by the shark was placed in the St. Louis papers. The people of St. Louis were happy to see that their Browns at least were going to enjoy some good fishing."

The site that Hedges and his board finally selected,

announcing their decision at a fractious meeting of stockholders back in St. Louis, was called Coffee Pot Bayou. No reasons for their choice were disclosed, but it's safe to guess that they liked the terms. The twenty-acre lot was offered rent-free for one year, with all holes filled and all stumps removed. At the end of the year the Browns could either give it back to the owners or buy it for $8,000, paying $3,000 down and 8 percent interest for the next five years. A contract was also arranged for the players' room and board, at $2.50 per player per day.

Thus spring training came to Florida as an institution. A wooden grandstand was built, the field was put in shape and presumably destumped, and on February 16, 1914, the Browns' manager, Branch Rickey, arrived in St. Petersburg with twenty players, four reporters and one photographer. The players were so glad to be warm, having left St. Louis in a snowstorm, that they went right out to the ballpark and loosened up. The next day Rickey put them to work in earnest, establishing a schedule that ran from eight-thirty to four-thirty every day except Sunday, with an hour out for lunch, and otherwise applying the principles of Christian abstinence for which, over the next half century, he came to be respected if not necessarily emulated.

"He forbade the playing of poker," Jabbo Gordon noted, "since it would keep the players up late. Liquor and cigarettes were not allowed. Rickey also ordered that no seconds on food would be allowed at meals. Since many boys had come from the farms, where one may eat his fill, they protested but to no avail. The reporters complained and won their point by sitting at a separate table.

"Some of the players were not very happy in St. Petersburg.

The movies closed at 9:30 and the one dance a week closed at 10:30. It had recently become a dry town and no saloons were open. Liquor was available at the Elks Club, but only one player was a member of that organization. To enjoy some night life several players visited Tampa, a more lively town across the bay. Unfortunately, they enjoyed Tampa too well occasionally and returned late the next day. This practice was viewed with alarm.''

Civic enthusiasm mounted as the players got ready for what was advertised as the first game ever played between major league teams in Florida, the other team being the Cubs. On opening day a half holiday was declared, businesses and schools were closed, and four thousand spectators turned up, some arriving by boat at a dock that had been built just for such waterborne fans. Special trains brought six hundred people from Tarpon Springs and Belleair. As for the game, the Cubs won it, 3-2. Evidently the Browns would need more than sunshine and good fishing.

Strictly, that wasn't the first foray into Florida by a major league club. In the spring of 1888 the Washington Statesmen (later the Senators) went to Jacksonville with fifteen players, including a young catcher named Connie Mack. Mack later recalled that he and his teammates were repeatedly turned away by hotels where they applied for rooms. The one that finally accepted them made the proviso that the players wouldn't mingle with the other guests or eat in the hotel dining room.

But it was the 1914 Browns who started the major leagues' Florida land rush. The baseball fever and the resulting increase in local business that they generated in St. Petersburg were not lost on tourist boards in other towns; maybe they could also get themselves a team. Their lure would be the priceless gift of sunshine, which the clubs were bound to find appealing. They were still stuck for their own spring training in such places as Wilmington, North Carolina; West Baden, West Virginia; Hot Springs, Arkansas; Mobile, Alabama; Augusta, Georgia; Charlottesville, Virginia; and Gulfport, Mississippi.

Every land rush needs a promoter, and the west coast of Florida found one in Al Lang, a Pittsburgh businessman who had moved to St. Petersburg in 1911 and embraced the town with such ardor that he eventually became mayor. Lang made it his mission to attract major league baseball to Florida, proceeding with such zeal that, by 1929, ten of the sixteen clubs had spring training camps there, including three in St. Petersburg—the Browns, the Boston Braves, who came from Galveston in 1922, and the New York Yankees, who came from New Orleans in 1925. The spot where the Yanks trained, Crescent Lake Park, is chiefly remembered because Babe Ruth hit a home run to right field that landed on the front porch of the West Coast Inn. Lang settled the Washington Senators in Tampa, the Brooklyn Dodgers in Clearwater, and the New York Giants in Sarasota, where, according to a contemporary sportswriter, Sam Crane, "nearly the whole team has had to buy real estate in order to get rid of the salesmen long enough to play a little baseball." Lang's reward was to have the new ballpark that was built in St. Petersburg in 1946 named for him, and two generations of fans making a tour of the Grapefruit League have contentedly sat in the sun at Al Lang Field ever since.

*

Of all the pleasant photographs in a paper-
back book called *Yesterday's Bradenton,* by Arthur C. Schofield,
which I bought at the newsstand of my Bradenton hotel as
soon as I checked in, the one I liked best shows Dizzy Dean
pumping gas at the service station he owned in the middle of
town. The St. Louis Cardinals trained in Bradenton from 1930
through 1936, and Dean joined the club in 1932 after winning
26 games for the Houston farm team the previous season. He
was just twenty-one. Every year the Cards would send Dean
to Bradenton several months before spring training began "so
he wouldn't get in any trouble back here in St. Louis." They
engaged a Bradenton sportswriter named Brack Cheshire to
look after their prize hillbilly until the rest of the team arrived—
surely one of the most unenviable assignments in the annals of
American sports.

In the photograph Dean looks as authentic as the palm trees
and the period cars and the Manatee River Hotel on Tenth
Street West. He is wearing the tidy uniform of a '30s gas station
attendant, including a visored cap, and is holding the nozzle of
a hose in the tank of a car. He is not, however, looking at the
nozzle; he is looking at the camera. Diz was no rube in matters
of publicity—he knew when to work the pumps. In any case,
it was enjoyable hoopla, and just seeing that photograph took
me back to my first years as a baseball fan—and my first awareness of the attachments that could form between a player from
rural America and the Florida town where his team alighted
for six weeks of spring training.

I remembered how I used to spread the sports section of the
New York Herald Tribune out on the rug (I was too small to
hold it open) and immerse myself in the exploits of Dean and

his brother Paul, Pepper Martin (the "Wild Horse of the Osage"), Leo Durocher, Frank Frisch, Joe ("Ducky") Medwick, and the other members of the Gas House Gang in far-off Bradenton. I had no idea what a gas house was, or what kind of gangs lived in them, but obviously they were high-spirited folk. (For that matter, what were Osages?) Dean, of course, would bring luster to the game in 1934, 1935 and 1936, winning 30, 28 and 24 games, before an arm injury abridged his career, just as later, announcing ballgames on the radio, he would bring luster to the American language with such usages as "slud" ("he slud into second base").

Now, in 1988, I had come to Bradenton myself to look for both its past and its present. Bradenton is twelve miles north of Sarasota, on Highway 41, the Tamiami Trail, which motorists have long used to traverse the Sunshine State. The two cities share an airport—it's called Bradenton-Sarasota—but they have almost nothing else in common. Sarasota is perched on the Gulf Coast, a coveted location for beach-house dwellers and condominium owners. Its downtown streets are suggestive of an old-money resort: boutiques, art galleries and pseudo-Spanish architecture. It's also one of the few places in Florida where culture is as sought-after as the sun. Many writers and artists live there, and daily sustenance is at hand in the form of museums, concert halls, theaters and a university. The look is one of affluence and self-esteem.

No such emanations are felt in Bradenton. It looks like the little brother who didn't get the inheritance. Most obviously, it just missed being a Gulf Coast town, having been settled instead along the mouth of the Manatee River. Manatees, or sea cows, were once abundant in the river and are still quite common. "Resort" and "leisure" aren't words that come to mind in Bradenton; words that come to mind are "hard work." If Sarasota's biggest attraction is the Ringling Museum of Art, Bradenton's biggest enterprise is the Tropicana factory, which processes a million gallons of orange juice a day. The company was founded in 1946 by Anthony T. Rossi, the traditional immigrant who arrived from Italy with the traditional few dollars in his pocket and credited his success to "God and America, who gave me everything I have." On my first night in Bradenton I was awakened at 3 A.M. by a long freight train clattering through the center of town, carrying orange juice (I assumed) to the far corners of America. I liked the sound.

Plain and poor from the beginning, Bradenton was not a place that said "This is it!" to Depression-era families driving down Highway 41 from the Midwest in search of a warmer home. Many of those '30s motorists had trailers hitched to their cars—Floridians called them "tin can tourists"—and were thus already provided with shelter and other necessities of life. It was a shame to let them get away. If only those families had a place to put their trailers—so the local boosters reasoned—they might settle down in Bradenton and never go back home. The economy could use their spending money.

Accordingly, in 1935, the chamber of commerce urged the city fathers to build a trailer park. The fathers declined, as city fathers will, but the Kiwanis Club rallied to the cause. In 1936 the club leased some land from the city, raised some money from Bradenton merchants, and built what would become "the world's largest trailer park," as a sign at its entrance proclaimed, with 1,190 spaces.

"You can't really be lonely unless you want to be," said Art Keller, the present manager, when I went around to see the park. An old photograph on his office wall showed the park as it appeared not long after it opened, a half century ago: a ragtag assortment of early cars and trailers, some of them so curvilinear that they look futuristic. Today, standardized and modernized, the Bradenton Trailer Park is a dense community of immobilized mobile homes, neatly arranged in a grid of streets, almost genteel. The descendants of the tin can tourists have put down roots.

"The only problem," Keller told me, "is that when newcomers arrive, they all want to have an orange tree, and we just can't allow that. They don't stop to think that that little orange tree is going to grow."

Such was Bradenton's early hospitality to the trailer nomads from the North that word got around, and today Manatee County has an estimated twenty thousand mobile homes. Their occupants, I imagined, would include some of the Bradentonians most eager for the Pirates to arrive every February.

*

To find the heart of Bradenton I went to the center of town. The heart, however, had been removed; everyone was at the De Soto Square Mall, an enclosed complex of one hundred–odd stores, including a Belk's and a J. C. Penney, three or four miles away in a former orange grove. (The mall is named for the Spanish explorer Hernando de Soto, who made his first landfall at what is now Bradenton in 1539.) On my stroll through the downtown streets I looked for the Dixie Grande Hotel, where, according to *Yesterday's Bradenton*, the members of the Cardinals' Gas House Gang "roamed the sitting room and played tricks on each other and the general public," but it was gone—torn down to save on taxes. Other vacant lots testified to other such deaths of unwanted taxable buildings. Dizzy Dean's gas station had been replaced by the Barnett Bank, and in the surrounding blocks I walked past many empty stores, their outside paint peeling, their windows empty except for a sign that said FOR LEASE. Taking a longer view, the First Baptist Church had a sign that said: THE LORD REIGNETH, LET THE EARTH REJOICE.

Only when I came to a row of buildings across from the Manatee County Courthouse did I find enterprises that were alive and well because they were needed right there—not out at the mall—for the lubrication of government: offices of attorneys, stenographers and court reporters; offices that provided abstracts, title insurance, legal services, accounting services and photocopies; offices of health, welfare and social service agencies, like the Manatee County Girls' Club ("where potential becomes reality"); the office of Andy Ireland, congressman of the 10th Congressional District, and C. J. Kristi's restaurant (OPEN 6 A.M.), where the day's special, for $1.50, was scrambled egg and slivered ham with homemade muffin. It had not been lost on Kristi's that a county government, like an army, marches on its stomach.

I went into Kristi's and had a cup of coffee at the counter. Across the street, a bus pulled up in front of the courthouse, and five or six people climbed on. I thought maybe they were going to Sarasota or St. Petersburg or Tampa for the afternoon. Then the bus turned, and I saw the sign announcing its destination: DE SOTO SQUARE MALL. I would have to find the heart of Bradenton somewhere else.

*

Bradenton started angling for a major league baseball team in 1920 and got its wish three years later. Someone on the board of trade made the propitious discovery that Sam Breadon, owner of the St. Louis Cardinals, owned some property up the Manatee River, and Breadon was persuaded to bring his club to Bradenton for spring training in 1923, relinquishing its previous camp in Orange, Texas. As an enticement the committee agreed to sell two thousand dollars' worth of tickets to the Cards' exhibition games, which it did. Crowds averaged between seven and eight hundred people.

The Cardinals stayed for two years and then jumped to Stockton, California, in 1925, and to San Antonio, Texas, in 1926. Loyalty to a spring training town was not yet part of the baseball ethic; on the contrary, it could be easily bought. After the Cards won their first pennant, in 1926, Avon Park, Florida, gave them a three-year guarantee, at fifteen thousand dollars a year, to train in that town. Breadon kept his part of the bargain, even though the Florida real estate boom had one of its periodic busts the following year, leaving Breadon with only the sparse gate receipts in 1928 and 1929. Thus it came about that the Cards returned to Bradenton in 1930 for the seven-year stay, one of the most picturesque in the history of spring training, that forever connected in baseball memory the city on the Manatee and the gang from the gas house.

Meanwhile, Bradenton had maintained its presence as a spring training site. The Phillies, who had been training in Leesburg, Virginia, came from 1925 through 1927, followed in 1928 and 1929 by the Red Sox, who had been in New Orleans. As for the post-Cardinal years, Casey Stengel's Boston Bees (as the Braves were then called) came from 1938 through

1940. During World War II, travel was curtailed and the clubs trained mostly in New Jersey and Indiana, but in 1948 life returned to Bradenton. The Boston Braves, their name restored, came for fifteen years, staying until 1962, by which time they had become the Milwaukee Braves. They were followed in 1963 by the Kansas City A's, who stayed until they moved west to Oakland in 1968 and decided to train nearer to their new constituency, at Mesa, Arizona. Thereupon the Bradenton city council put an end to fickle romances and in 1969 signed a forty-year lease—a contract of unprecedented length—with the Pirates, who had been discontented in Fort Myers, Florida, and the Bucs have been there ever since.

Over that sixty-five-year span of Bradenton baseball, countless players who became stars of brightest wattage, besides Diz, took their first major league spring training at McKechnie Field. Today it's hard to think that any of them were ever rookies. But facts are facts, especially in baseball, and the records show, for instance, that Hank Aaron came up to the Braves in 1954, Catfish Hunter and Reggie Jackson joined the A's in 1965 and 1967, respectively, and Dave Parker reported to the Pirates in 1973.

*

I got to Bradenton for spring training two weeks after the Pirates did, just when they were moving their base of operations from "Pirate City," their training complex on the outskirts of town, to McKechnie Field, where they would continue to train in the mornings and play their four-week schedule of exhibition games with other major league clubs in the afternoons. Until quite recently, baseball organizations trained their major and minor league clubs in different towns—some owners thought the veterans would be a bad influence on the rookies—and when a player finally made it to a major league camp, after long servitude on Southern ballfields of minimal comfort and charm, it was a high moment in his career. Today the trend is to consolidate all the clubs in one location and to ply them with the same principles of instruction and fitness, thereby exposing every player in the system to the philosophy of the parent club and exposing every manager, coach and instructor to the total pool of talent.

Pirate City was built jointly by the Pittsburgh club and the city of Bradenton when they signed their forty-year lease, on 160 acres of land that had once been the city dump. Its access road, Twenty-seventh Street East, was paved and renamed Roberto Clemente Memorial Drive. The main structure in the complex looks like a motel that somehow got combined with the administration building of a community college—and, in fact, that's essentially what it is; it perfectly embodies baseball's new corporate efficiency. The building has seventy-two rooms that can house 220 players—married players may rent their own lodgings in the Bradenton area—plus a cafeteria, executive offices, conference rooms, lounges, press facilities and other such amenities. Beyond the building is a clubhouse, an array of pitching machines and sliding pits, and four baseball diamonds that fan out from a central observation tower, where observers can look down on players batting at four different home plates.

Baseball fans touring the Grapefruit League are welcome to attend these sweaty rites of spring, which begin around February 20. But only a diehard would appreciate such rudimentary toil. Most tourists don't come to Bradenton until after March 1. By that time the squad which in some combination will constitute the Pirates—a fifty-man roster consisting of the previous season's regulars and the most highly rated prospects—has moved to McKechnie Field. One reason for waiting, of course, is that the fans will see actual games and not mere workouts. The other reason is McKechnie Field itself; the ballpark is widely regarded as the ideal of what a spring training park ought to look like and feel like—at least for spectators.

Its old-fashioned virtues are honorably earned, dating back to 1923. That's when the city built the wooden grandstand as a spring training site for the Cardinals, named it City Park, and opened it with an airborne flourish. According to Kent Chetlain, a Manatee County commissioner and a compulsive baseball archivist, the commissioner of baseball, Kenesaw Mountain Landis, always wintered at the Bellevue Biltmore Hotel in Clearwater. "A Bradenton auto dealer named Harry Land, who was also an aviator," Chetlain told me, "flew over to the Biltmore, landed on its golf course, picked up Landis and brought him back here for the opening ceremonies. A brass band was playing out on the diamond to welcome him."

City Park was subsequently known as Ninth Street Park and as Braves Field, and it got its present name in 1962 when Bradenton decided to honor its longtime resident Bill McKechnie upon his induction into the Baseball Hall of Fame. In his twenty-five-year managing career "Deacon Bill" managed four National League clubs and brought off the unique feat of winning pennants for three of them: the 1925 Pirates, the 1928 Cardinals, and the 1939 and 1940 Reds. McKechnie so liked

Bradenton that he bought a home there, lived there, retired there and died there in 1965. Thus he furnished Bradenton with one of its two household gods, the second one being the great outfielder Edd Roush, another longtime resident, who was elected to the Baseball Hall of Fame at the same time as McKechnie.

The years were not as kind to McKechnie Field as they were to Deacon Bill's memory. "It's the closest thing to a cow pasture I've seen," said Whitey Herzog after bringing his Royals there in 1979. The Royals outfielder Hal MacRae said it reminded him of an Iowa cornfield, and the Pirates' Dave Parker said that "playing the outfield was like playing in a potato patch." The infield was no less rural in its associations— Willie Stargell said, "You just can't tell what kind of hop you're going to get"—and several other players, fearful of abrasions, complained about the tin fence in the outfield, which had "things sticking out, like nails and screws."

Stung by these critiques, the city set about bringing the field up to proper standards in the early 1980s. Today no bucolic allusions are made to the outfield, infield hops are true, and the fence beyond the warning track threatens no loss of blood. Much of the money for the renovation was provided by the local Pirates Boosters Club. I wanted to know more about those Boosters; if I was looking for the heart of the relationship between the Pirates and Bradenton, that was obviously the place to look. But first I wanted to see McKechnie Field on my own. Deacon Bill himself was firmly fixed in my memory—a gray-haired gentleman, almost as old as Connie Mack, who brought his finely tuned Cincinnati teams to the Polo Grounds to bury my boyhood Giants in the late '30s. (I now realize that he was little over fifty at the time.) I drove out Ninth Street West from the center of town. It was a blue-collar street, the kind that has auto body shops. After eight or nine blocks I saw a structure on the left that unmistakably said "grandstand" and a sign that said:

McKECHNIE FIELD
SOUTHERN HOME OF
THE PITTSBURGH PIRATES

The time was late afternoon; everything was closed for the day. I got out and peered through the fence. McKechnie Field was, as reputed, a gem. It had three sections of dark green covered stands—behind home plate and behind first and third base—with open wooden bleachers extending beyond them down the first- and third-base lines. The field was immaculate: green grass that smelled as good as it looked. Enclosing the outfield was a low fence that didn't appear to have nails and screws sticking out. A billboard in left field said:

BRADENTON
"The Friendly City"
A Little Bit of Paradise

The scoreboard in left-center field was designed to tell me the line score of the game and nothing else. There would be no video replays; I would have to see what I saw when I saw it and never again. There would be no waterfalls, no flashing signs exhorting me to cheer; on the contrary, I had the feeling that an occasional nap in the Florida sun would be excused and even encouraged. The concession stands had signs announcing that what they sold were hot dogs, beer and soda. A sign outside the ticket window said GENERAL ADMISSION $3.00. CHILDREN $1.00. Cities couldn't get friendlier than that.

I had seen the past and it worked. In the morning the Pirates would be there for spring training, and so would I.

CHAPTER 4

The Gospel According to Thrift

To see a dying major league franchise being nursed back to health is one of the most satisfying spectacles in American sport—and American business. The story almost always has at its center one person of unusual character and gifts—a Branch Rickey, a Larry MacPhail, a Frank Cashen—and it also has just enough mystery to make it unteachable in any school of management. The mystery can be summed up in one word: intuition. All the great club-builders know talent when they see it and will risk their reputation on what they think they see.

They also have patience—the patience to wait for the talent to mature. They believe in the farm system: the historic structure of minor league clubs that keep replenishing the major league club with talent. They also believe in education; teaching is a sacred charge, and the men they appoint as managers, coaches and instructors throughout the organization are men who share that ideal. They also know that money can buy only so much—that cash is better spent on the system than on the superstar. It was no accident that Frank Cashen's champion New York Mets of 1986, like his champion Baltimore Orioles of the 1970s, had grown their own Strawberrys and Goodens and allowed them to ripen, while the plutocratic Yankees, spending tens of millions of dollars to hire established stars, still hadn't bought themselves a pennant in more than a decade. Wisdom in a general manager is trusting the system, not trying to beat it.

These thoughts were in my mind when I got my first look at the Pirates out on McKechnie Field. They had the earmarks of a club in the early stages of a classic rebuilding. Seen close, the players were very young. They weren't "athletes"; they were everybody's brother, not long out of high school, full of the energy that boys not long out of high school assume they will have forever. Coaches were drilling the players in relays, cutoffs, pickoffs and other collaborative plays. I would want to talk to those coaches about their teaching methods, and to the manager, Jim Leyland, and to the players themselves.

But first I hoped I could meet Syd Thrift. His was the philosophy that had shaped the club I would be writing about. I didn't know if general managers even came to spring training. Probably Thrift was at his desk in Pittsburgh, doing paperwork and making phone calls. I asked someone standing at the railing who looked Pirate-connected whether Thrift was expected at any time.

"That's Syd right over there," he said, pointing toward first base. A Pirate player was talking with someone who looked like a field hand in an old movie about the rural South—a heavy man in his late fifties, well over six feet tall, with a big head, black hair and a drooping, somewhat mournful face. He was wearing farmer's clothes. At regular intervals he leaned over to spit out a gob of something that would be advertised on the side of a barn in North Carolina, and when he started ambling toward the railing, moving slowly, as if his feet hurt, I heard a drawl that came from deepest Dixie. It took me back to my army basic training at Camp Lee, Virginia.

I introduced myself to him, and the mournful face rearranged itself into a smile—a country-boy affability that stopped short of inviting the stranger home for lunch. I asked if he had any time to talk to me; no exhibition game was being played that afternoon. He thought about his schedule for the day—a radio interview, a civic luncheon in Bradenton, two business conferences—and finally said he would meet me at three o'clock. Somehow I didn't expect him to remember.

*

At three o'clock Thrift wandered out onto the field. By the time he got to first base, where I caught up with him, he had talked to half a dozen people. This was no hands-off general manager—he was a man minutely involved in the lives of his players and his coaches. He led me across the grass to right field, where we sat on the bullpen bench. Just in front of us, pitchers were working out with catchers. Beyond them, outfielders were chasing long flies and throwing to relay men in the infield. Occasionally Thrift called to one of the players. He was so totally in his element that I now couldn't picture him behind a desk in Pittsburgh. I asked him what spring training means to the club.

"Preparation," he said. He let the word linger: the biblical text for the day. "Anything you want to undertake, preparation is absolutely vital: how well you prepare physically and how well you prepare mentally. We try to make certain that our players are prepared for the championship season. First comes their physical conditioning. We begin with a diagnostic approach: the evaluation of their muscular system with the Cybex machine and the evaluation of their visual system by Dr. William A. Harrison. That's followed by a program to correct the weaknesses and develop the strengths that we've found.

"Another part of our overall program is to give the players an awareness of drugs, alcohol, AIDS—whatever we can grasp. Because I believe that knowledge is a vital thing. In the Book of Hosea it says, 'My children shall perish for lack of knowledge,' and I believe totally in that philosophy. I believe that the more a person is informed, the better he feels about himself. Because success in this business is based on the confidence level of the player. All these young men are blessed with special physical talents, and if you put them on a scale you'd find that a lot of it is relative. They may be outstanding runners, they may be outstanding throwers, they may be outstanding fielders, they may have outstanding body control. But what makes one player a winning player and one a losing player?"

The sentences were rolling out, rotund and perfectly formed. I had the feeling that I was not the first person to hear them.

"There are two crucial elements," Thrift continued. "One is desire. The other is endurance: stick-to-itiveness. If you don't have a tremendous desire to excel you can't make it, and if you don't have a tough mental attitude you also can't make it, because in baseball you fail more than you succeed. If you fail seven times out of ten you hit .300, and if you hit .300 you go to the Hall of Fame. It's a question of learning how to handle failure. How do you see failure? Do you see it as the end of everything? Or do you see it as an opportunity to do something great?"

After every sentence Thrift leaned over and performed an act of expectoration that matched the sentence in the deliberateness of its delivery.

"So all those things are vital," Thrift went on, "and to make them work you have to thoroughly evaluate your players as you acquire them: their makeup, their disposition, their attitudes. Because out of all that comes a thing that we call spirit. That spirit is like the wind: you can't see it, but you can see the results of it." Thrift pointed to a flagpole in the outfield. "Do you see that flag moving? You don't see anything making it move. That's what spirit is like in the clubhouse—I can't begin to tell you how important it is. I ask the players a simple commonsense question: 'Which is more important, the soil or the seed?' The answer is the soil. Because you can have the finest hybrid seed in the world, and if you throw it right there"—he pointed to a cement path next to the bench—"it ain't gonna grow on that cement. But the soil is conditioned daily."

I had heard these cadences before—these rushing torrents of persuasion—coming from the pulpits of small churches in the South. "But even if the soil is great," Thrift went on, "there are weeds and moles and reptiles, and weasels that get in the chicken coop, and you have to learn how to identify them. We've got a lot of weasels around now, I can tell you that. These players are on stage, and the whole world is attempting

to sell them something. My father used to say, 'The world's a
barbershop and everybody's trying to shave you.' That's why
we also teach these boys things down here like personal finance.
Because in the Bible money is mentioned more than any other
subject. More than three hundred times. So here they are, and
they're all striving to get money, and what are they gonna do
with it? They ain't gonna make much money at the dog track.
Not as much as they think. Not even if they own the dog.''

I enjoyed this economics lesson, and Thrift enjoyed my
enjoyment of it. Barry Bonds came over and joined us on the
bench. Thrift put his arm around him, and the two sat together
companionably—the twenty-three-year-old outfielder and the
fifty-nine-year-old boss. ''I try to spend time with the players
and make them aware of the hazards they'll be running into,''
Thrift said. ''I remember Barry's first TV show. We spent
about an hour in my hotel room in Los Angeles, and I told
him, 'On the radio you can duck a little, but on TV you're
right there in front of the good Lord and the world, and most
interviewers are going to ask you one question that will throw
you for a loop. Now, how are you going to deal with that
question? You've got different ways. You can either change the
subject, or you can get them to repeat the question while you
get yourself together—because it's *coming!*—or you can answer
the question with a question.' Well, it came—do you
remember, Barry?''

''I sure do,'' Bonds said. ''It was really below the belt.''

''They do it to me, too,'' Thrift said, ''and it just infuriates
me. So you've got to handle it. You can't just all of a sudden
crack the guy on the head.''

*

Thrift grew up in a place called Locust Hill, in the Tidewater part of Virginia, not far from Chesapeake Bay and the Rappahannock River. "A lot of people made their living from the water, so never a day goes by when I'm not constantly aware of wind direction," Thrift said. He admires his fellow Virginian Thomas Jefferson for keeping accurate daily weather records at Monticello. Thrift's father ran a general merchandise store—"he sold everything from toothpicks to horse collars"—and the family lived on a small farm. Syd junior was eager to get away; only later did he realize that to grow up in rural America and meet all the people who hang around a country store is a rich education. His mother had been a schoolteacher. After her marriage she helped at the store, but she also taught Thrift and his two younger sisters, the result being, he said, that "when I got to first grade they found that I could read all these books and do all this arithmetic. So they put me in second grade, which made everybody in that class mad as hell at me." Thus accelerated, he graduated from high school at sixteen and from Randolph-Macon College at twenty. "I never have known why we were in such a hurry or where we were going," he said. "My mother is eighty-three now and she's still got this tremendous attitude about learning. She's just gone back to taking piano lessons."

After college, where he was an all-state southpaw on the baseball team, Thrift was signed by the Yankees in 1949 as a pitcher and a first baseman. He was sent to La Grange, Georgia, a club in the nethermost regions of the Yankees' farm system. In January of 1950 he was invited to Phoenix to attend the first instructional school the Yankees had ever held. It was run by Casey Stengel and his Yankees coaching staff, which included Bill Dickey, Frank Crosetti and Jim Turner. The idea was to bring all the top prospects in the Yankees' minor league system together in one camp. "Billy Martin was my roommate," Thrift recalled, "and some of the other guys were Mickey Mantle, Gil McDougald and Lew Burdette. The talent in that one place was awesome. I learned so much about teaching and learning from that coaching staff. They spent an awful lot of time teaching defense. There wasn't a day when defense wasn't taught and baserunning wasn't taught. Over and over and over again. And catching. I watched how Bill Dickey drilled the catchers on blocking balls. Over and over."

Thrift's next two ballplaying years were spent in the army. He got out in 1953, had another minor league tryout before a sore arm put an end to his dreams, and then became a teacher and a coach at Mount Vernon High School, in Alexandria, Virginia, teaching history, government and general science. Simultaneously he attended graduate school at George Washington University, studying secondary education, and coached American Legion teams. "I was always trying to keep busy," he said.

Keeping busy turned out to have been a good thing to do: in 1956 he caught the eye of Rex Bowen, the Pittsburgh Pirates' scouting supervisor for the Middle Atlantic States— and, incidentally, the man who signed the immortal Mazeroski. Bowen had seen Thrift's high school and American Legion teams play and was impressed by his judgment; he asked Thrift to help him run some tryout games. "He was a very intelligent man, methodical and highly organized," Thrift said, "and he had key people that he depended on. Watching how he operated taught me a lot." In 1957 Bowen was promoted to scouting director of the Pirates, and Thrift was the first person he hired. He was brought to Pittsburgh to meet Joe L. Brown, the Pirates' general manager, and was assigned to the Midwest. He had never been in the Midwest and was nervous about being in a new territory, with people different from those he had known, and "with only a reasonable facsimile of an idea" of what he was supposed to do. "I found the Midwestern people absolutely unbelievable—warm and receptive and straight and honest. They went out of their way to help me, especially the older established baseball scouts."

So began eleven years as a Pirate scout—years that were pivotal to Thrift's later career. Rex Bowen and Joe L. Brown were both disciples of Branch Rickey, who had been the Pirates' general manager from 1951 through 1956, and they ingrained in Thrift the principles that have come to be generically known as the Rickey system. Rickey had a Christian missionary's faith in education, potential and character. He was a shrewd judge and nurturer of talent and a man who acted boldly on his beliefs. It was no quirk of history that Rickey was the chosen or self-chosen instrument for breaking baseball's color line, in 1947, when he was general manager of the Brooklyn Dodgers and brought Jackie Robinson up to the major leagues.

Thrift became a quick student of the scouting arts, learning to evaluate talent at different levels of different minor leagues as far west as North Dakota, in such Northern League cities as Aberdeen, St. Cloud, Winnipeg and Duluth. Some of the players he signed, including Al Oliver, Woodie Fryman, Jerry May and Bob Robertson, would help Pittsburgh win two World Series and six division titles in the 1970s. But after eleven years Thrift felt the itch to try something new, and in

1968 he went to work for Ewing Kauffman, a millionaire who had just bought a franchise called the Kansas City Royals in the newly expanded American League.

It is in the nature of expansion clubs that they are born with no players and with no farm system to supply them; the roster gets filled with castaways from other major league teams, and the club duly starts life by repeatedly finishing last. Few scenarios in American business are more discouraging. To Thrift, however, the very idea was thrilling. "Imagine! A chance to start a new team with nothing!" he said. "What it required was a lot of scouting and a lot of knowledge, and I was thankful that I had seen all those players and all those teams and all those leagues. Because when you capture a person such as myself to work for you, you have acquired a lot of knowledge of things that have passed, but also of things of the future. Just the other day I told someone that when we finish the free-agent draft this year, 1988, we will have signed players for the Pittsburgh franchise for 1992 and 1993. How many people in other areas of baseball do more long-range work than someone who goes out and signs players who aren't ready for the major leagues— I mean they're not even *close* to being ready—and starts training them?

"I did a lot to put the Kansas City Royals together, because I had seen the greatest number of players. I had seen them from the Carolina League to the Southern League to the International League. I had seen the Dick Dragos and the Lou Piniellas and could recommend them. Any time you find a veteran scout who has seen so many players and has complete records on all of them, it's like finding a bag with a lot of money in it. Somebody once asked me whether I'd rather have a superstar player or a superscout—I mean a really productive scout—and I said, 'I'll take the scout, because he's got a chance to get me more than one player. If I get one superstar, that's all I have.' "

Thrift and Kauffman were impatient with the usual methods of obtaining talent. Surely the country was full of good ballplayers who hadn't been drafted and just weren't being looked for, Thrift told Kauffman. He had signed some of them himself—players such as Don Money. Their radical solution was to found a school—the Royals Baseball Academy, in Sarasota, with Thrift as its director. He sent a letter to 16,000 high school coaches, asking them to suggest candidates, and over the next three years 7,682 boys were enrolled and given tryouts. One of them was Frank White, who made it to the parent Royals in 1973 and has been at second base ever since. Another was the shortstop U. L. Washington, who played alongside White from 1978 to 1984.

With so many guinea pigs at his disposal, Thrift turned into the closest thing to a mad scientist that baseball has yet spawned, bringing to his campus a steady procession of physicists, time-lapse photographers, ballistics engineers, meteorologists, optometrists, audiologists, physiologists and psychologists to try to prove (often with peculiar-looking machines) his belief that the human animal can be trained to see a ball better, throw it harder, get off to a faster running start and feel more emotionally fit than had previously been supposed. "I just opened the doors," Thrift recalled, "and let all these crazy people in." Thereby he got his first taste of what it is like to be laughed at by the baseball establishment, and three years later the academy closed—by no means the first progressive school in America to be mocked to an early grave. But some of the crazies turned out to have been making sense; today many diagnostic techniques that were pioneered at Thrift's academy are routinely used throughout baseball in player development. As for the parent Kansas City Royals, who started from scratch, by the mid-1970s they had become the most consistent winners in the American League's western division.

*

The final chunk of experience that would prepare Thrift for his present job—executive management—fell into place in 1975 when he was hired by Charley Finley, the mercurial owner of the Oakland A's. "When you worked for Finley you had a chance to do everything," Thrift said. "You signed the players to big-league contracts, you were the scouting director, you were the farm director—you were *it*, because he had all the titles but you were the one who was there every day. Charley was very good to me. I attended every owners' meeting with him; I attended every general managers' meeting with him, or for him, and every scouting directors' meeting and every farm directors' meeting. When we went to the winter meetings it was just the two of us. I look at the clubs today, checking into a hotel with twenty-five or thirty people, and I laugh, because I was with the Charley Finley Show once, and it was he and me. Mostly he."

When the advent of free agency began to dismantle those championship A's, Thrift left the Charley Finley Show. Seeing no other jobs in the marketplace, he quit baseball and started a real estate business in Vienna, Virginia, thus generating the disdainful charge that would greet his appointment to his present job in 1985—that he had long been out of the game.

But Thrift considers his realty years no less instructive than his earlier jobs. "I learned much that I needed to know about finance," he said, "and I also learned about human nature. Real estate and baseball are very much alike. You're making judgments about people and gambling on how well you evaluate them."

Nor did he abandon his first love. He found ways to keep busy—notably, when he accompanied an all-star American high school baseball team on a three-week goodwill tour of Sweden, Denmark and Finland in 1981. His son Jim was one of the all-stars, and Thrift went along as clinic coordinator. The player who most excited him was an eighteen-year-old outfielder and first baseman from the Bronx named Bobby Bonilla. "I ran him sixty yards and clocked him at six point eight," Thrift recalled. He also liked Bonilla's arm, his power as a switch-hitter, and his ability to play every position where Thrift tried him, especially third base. Back home, he persuaded the Pittsburgh organization, with whom he no longer had any ties, to sign the kid from the Bronx, and the rest is, as they say, history— probably the only time American baseball history has been made in Scandinavia.

Bonilla and Thrift were reunited on the Pirates in 1986. No miracles were wrought overnight. Bonilla, shuffled between first base, the outfield and the bench, was an inconsistent hitter, seemingly needing a regular spot in the lineup. In mid-1987 Thrift gave him one: third base. While the coaches went to work on his fielding, Bonilla went to work with his bat, leading the club in hitting and runs batted in after the All-Star break and hitting home runs from both sides of the plate, including one that landed in the upper deck of Three Rivers Stadium, where only six had ever landed before. (Willie Stargell hit four of them.)

As for how Thrift himself got back to the Pirates, his patron was Joe L. Brown. The club's longtime general manager had been coaxed out of retirement by the new owners, desperate for advice on how to salvage the property they had bought. As acting general manager, Brown took it as his first priority to replace himself. He remembered the country boy he had dispatched into the alien corn of the Midwest as a scout thirty years before and whose labors with Kansas City and Oakland he had followed ever since. He told the board he knew the man for the job.

*

Barry Bonds had long since left us on the bullpen bench, but several other players had taken his place, dropping in briefly on Thrift's chronicle. I had been struck by the exactness of his memory for dates, places, names and numbers—a scout's memory, perhaps. I was also beginning to get the point of the man; his story added up. What at first had sounded like a Baptist preacher's hyperbole turned out to be a life of solid achievements. If the achievements were perhaps slightly magnified, so was Thrift himself. I liked the confidence behind the life—the willingness to act on deeply felt intuitions. I also liked the man. The melodious drawl did its work quietly; humor was never far away.

I asked Thrift how he had selected Jim Leyland as the Pirate manager. "First," he said, "it had to be someone who had a complete understanding of all the things that are necessary to

manage. I knew that Jim Leyland had spent *his* time in preparation with years of minor league managing at all levels, from
the rookie league through successful years of Triple A. I also
knew from his record that he was a good leader—a good
manager of people. Also, he'd had four years of coaching third
base for the White Sox under Tony LaRussa. That all gave
him a blend of experience that nobody else had. Among other
things, those years with the White Sox gave him an insight
into how to answer questions from the media, which is very
important for a major league manager.

"I also felt that the manager of the Pirates should be someone
who reflected the work ethic of the Pittsburgh area—someone
who you knew was a hardworking guy. With Jim that comes
across real quick. I also wanted someone who would be able to
relate to younger players, because I knew that if we were going
to improve we had to switch our plan of attack and place a
much greater emphasis on young people. Most of all, I knew
that Jim would be open-minded and receptive to new ideas. I
didn't want some retread or old-guard guy who had his own
fixed way of doing things. That eliminated a gross multitude.

"I told them all up front: 'I'm a hands-on general manager.'
On other clubs the general manager never goes on the field. I
said, 'I can't do what everybody else does. There are no territories with me.' As human beings we should be one step above
animals, and we should be one step above territories. But in
corporations and everywhere else, everybody's got these little
territories. It becomes nothing but politics, and creativity is
nonexistent. If you can't use the mind you've been given, that's
a sad state of affairs." Thrift didn't mention that territorial
rights mattered greatly to him at the end of the 1987 season.
Riding high on the club's final streak and resentful that presi-

dent Malcolm "Mac" Prine insisted on having final authority in day-to-day baseball decisions, he forced a showdown with the Pittsburgh board of directors. The board sided with Thrift in the power play, and Prine was ousted.

Thrift picked up a baseball that had rolled under the bench and held it up, gripping it with his two fingers across the seams where they are farthest apart, not with his two fingers resting on the seams where they are closest together.

"We've found with our tests," he said, "that if a pitcher throws a four-seam fastball—holding it like this—it will go two to four miles an hour faster than a two-seam fastball. Think of that! You can improve a pitcher's performance just by changing the way he holds the ball! We've gone farther in our research than any organization in baseball, and we've only begun to scratch the surface. I started that research at the Royals Baseball Academy, and now I'm having it transferred into learning for the Pittsburgh club."

To listen to Thrift on the subject of the four-seam fastball was not unlike listening to the man who invented the wheel. He gloried in explaining the principles that result in those two to four extra miles per hour. I asked him whether most of the Pirates' research is related to the aerodynamics of the ball itself.

"That's only a small part of it," he said. "We have a track specialist down here from George Mason University, Frank Raines, who has also worked with the Washington Redskins. He's teaching us running: running form, first and second steps, how to improve. That's an integral part of offensive and defensive baseball. We also make our baserunners aware of the pitcher's delivery; we have it measured with stopwatches, and we know exactly how many feet you're supposed to be off each base. Then there's Dr. William Harrison and his visual systems approach, which is designed to improve your concentration on what you see. The human body has five systems—touch, smell, seeing, hearing and feeling—and in baseball the most important one is your visual system. It's responsible for eighty percent of your total performance. We know we can train that visual system to be better by not letting the audio system interfere— by not letting what you hear affect what you see. Because it does. Everything affects everything else. Some people are sensitive to wind, for example. I personally don't like wind; I don't even go bird-hunting on windy days—it just messes up my mind."

Science notwithstanding, I was still left with the mystery of intuition. What was this sixth sense—this ability to evaluate talent?

"I really don't know," Thrift said. "I've had a gift, as long as I can remember, the way other people have a gift for art or music. I can look at a player and see his strengths and his weaknesses. That's not unusual—many people can see a player's flaws. But I can also see the solution. It's like a camera and a computer combined. What I see that's wrong in a player may be just a slight thing—something about his hands, or his feet, or the angle of his bat—and it's like a bell going off. Most of the time I can see the solution immediately, but often it takes twenty-four hours. Sometimes it comes at four o'clock in the morning—I wake up with a perfect answer to the problem. Isn't that amazing?"

I asked Thrift what he does with these revelations. He said he takes them to the manager and the coaches. I put it to him that he must have an exceptional relationship with those men; technical advice from the front office in any line of work is seldom received kindly by the skilled help.

"I do—I have very special people," Thrift agreed. "And I don't know all the answers. Sometimes I go to my coaches and I say, 'What do *you* see?' And they'll give me a clue and I'll say, 'Doggone, that's exactly right!' The main thing is you've got to know what you're looking for. If you don't know the difference between a crow and a duck you don't mess with no duck-hunting."

*

The afternoon had ebbed away. Thrift's talent was dispersed across McKechnie Field. Some of it was big-league talent now; some wouldn't be ready until tomorrow or the day after. I felt that he could put a sticker on every uniform: 1989, 1990, 1991. Thrift won't allow the people who work for him to use pens. Pen users, he says, tend to make indelible decisions, and with baseball players nothing is indelible. He insists on pencils with good erasers as standard equipment for his staff.

"See that kid?" Thrift said, pointing to a skinny outfielder. "His name is Wes Chamberlain. He's got a lot of ability. We signed him last year from Mississippi Southern, and he played for our club in Watertown, New York, which is a *long* way from the big leagues. And yet it's close—I want to put that idea in his head. I brought him over here today from Pirate City, where our minor leaguers train, because I want him to see the environment for himself. I want him to be on the same field as the Pirate regulars and to get his turn in the batting cage. I want him to realize that the major leagues is not as far away as he thinks it is. It's not some little lightning bug way off in Altoona."

CHAPTER 5

Going to Work

On the bulletin board in the Pirates' clubhouse, just outside the trainer's room, I saw an announcement that said:

MARCH 24 PARTY
AT SANDBAR RESTAURANT
FOR ALL PLAYERS & STAFF (AND FAMILIES)
FREE RIBS, CHICKEN & REFRESHMENTS
PLEASE SIGN UP BELOW

"Those people hold that party for us every year," said Kent Biggerstaff, the Pirate trainer, when I asked him if this was an annual event, "and it's always a lot of fun." The invitation reinforced my first impression of the clubhouse as a home—a large living room where the players could come and go as a family, in relative privacy and calm.

But that image was only partly right. Most of all, the clubhouse was an office. It was the place where the manager and the coaches and the players went to work every day. In this clubhouse in Bradenton and in their home clubhouse at Three Rivers Stadium in Pittsburgh and in the visitors' clubhouse in every city in the National League, they would put on their uniforms more than two hundred times. They would read their mail, give interviews, autograph baseballs and transact countless other details of their profession. It was in the clubhouse at McKechnie Field that I stopped thinking of baseball as a game and started thinking of it as a job. I saw how much discipline these men would need to just show up for work every day: to sustain a high level of physical and mental competence through 42 days of spring training, 162 games of championship play, and thousands of hours of tedium incurred in riding in planes, getting to the airport and the ballpark, and waiting around hotels.

The clubhouse at McKechnie Field was strikingly neat—there was none of the detritus of old socks and wet towels that I expected. Fifty open cubicles formed the perimeter of the room, each one hung with several sets of clean uniforms, heaped with different kinds of baseball shoes, and supplied with fresh T-shirts and other athletic gear. In the middle of the room a few weights stood ready for any player in fear of fat. Watching over it all was John Hallahan, the club's equipment manager since 1957, who started with the Pirates in 1947 as a batboy. Often there was music: a radio tuned to moderate rock. The only other link to the outside world was a wall telephone; life's routine crises wait for no man, whatever his job. I heard one player, recently acquired by the club and still in mid-negotiation for a house in the Pittsburgh area, giving instructions to his wife or his realtor. "If we only had to pay one and

a half points," he said, "we could go with the eight and a half
percent adjustable rate mortgage." It used to be that if a
ballplayer was talking in numerical language on the telephone
he was playing the horses.

*

       Because none of the players were stars, I
didn't at first know any of them by sight. The only one who
stood out from the others was pitcher Bob Walk, the grand-
daddy of the club at thirty-one. He was a familiar type: the
older boy at camp who has been around for so many summers
that he has a kidding relationship with the counselors. He was
the classic overgrown kid, big and happy-go-lucky. I asked him
if he was feeling the burdens of being an elder statesman.

       "I try to talk to the players who have never been in the big
leagues before," he said. "They're a little bit on the intimidated
side, and I try to smooth things along for them. I don't really
consider myself an older player—usually people in my role are
pushing forty. But since there's no one else around to do it, I
talk to the young guys and tell them that if they're going to be
successful up here they've got to do the same things that got
them here. They can't be intimidated—especially off the field
and around the clubhouse. They have to be the same as they've
always been. I tell them, 'You wouldn't be here if you didn't
have the talent. So you can't be so uptight and scared that your
talent doesn't come across.'

       "I've found myself to be interested in what some of them
do—what their lives are like. In years past I haven't paid much
attention to that. But this year I don't have to worry so much

about trying to make the team, just about getting in shape. So I go out of my way to make these kids feel at home and talk to them, just about dumb stuff, trying to make them think, 'Hey, everybody up here's the same, especially on this team.' I let them know that if they do their job, no matter what level they're at now, eventually they're going to get their chance to play in the big leagues."

Another relative veteran was the outfielder R. J. Reynolds, who came up to the Dodgers in 1983 and was now, at twenty-six, in his sixth major league spring training clubhouse. "Spring training has a lot to do with the type of team you're playing with," he said, "and how far along it has come: Is it a rebuilding process or is it an established club? Either way, when you first arrive it's the same thing—getting loose, trying to get the little cracks and kinks out. If you play enough years you've already done something during the winter to get yourself ready, so this is like a refresher course. You're here to polish up your different skills and go over your different plays. But wherever you live— my wife and I rent a house out at Holmes Beach—you have a time to get to the ballpark. You have work to do. Sometimes you also have work to do after the game. It could be taking extra ground balls, it could be bunting, it could be execution: for example, how to manufacture runs without getting hits. You do a lot of that—you work on execution.

"Basically, you shouldn't be under any pressure, because the atmosphere here in spring training is so nice. For the rookies, of course, it's different. I can remember my first year. You're always trying to figure out the roster—who's going to make the team—and that can get in the way of your performance, because you're not loose in games. It's also hard on the manager and the coaches, because they're the ones who have to tell a young player, 'Well, son, you can play this game, but we don't have any room for you, so just stay sharp and we'll be calling on you.' ''

One day I got an inkling of what that dismal moment would be like. I noticed a boy sitting in front of a locker who looked like a high school senior. I thought he was somebody's kid brother, in town for a visit. But then he began to put on a uniform, one that had a high number: number 63. I sneaked a look at the media guide and found that number 63 was a twenty-three-year-old pitcher named Mike York, who had already knocked around the minor leagues for five years: in Oneonta, Sarasota, Bristol, Lakeland, Gastonia and Macon. His league-leading won-and-lost average (17–6) for Macon in the South Atlantic League in 1987 had presumably earned him a major league tryout this winter. He reminded me of the kind of rookie Ring Lardner wrote about—slightly stunned, expecting nothing, grateful for anything.

"It's an awesome feeling," he told me, "being in the Pirates' camp with the best guys and having crowds watch you work out. I was overwhelmed when I got here. But it's fun. I've been in minor league spring training camps for the last five years. In those camps you've got maybe a hundred and seventy guys. Those coaches know what they're doing, but they just can't give you much individual attention. But here you've got five or six coaches and only forty or fifty guys, so you get much more one-on-one instruction. Ray Miller, the pitching coach, has been working with me a lot. He just takes you aside and works with you. He just wants you to be yourself."

Another rookie I approached in the clubhouse was Vicente

Palacios, a tall, strong, twenty-four-year-old right-hander from Mexico. I had watched him working out with catcher Mike LaValliere and had liked his speed and his fluid rhythm. He was much farther along than Mike York: as a starting pitcher for the Pirates' Triple A Vancouver club in 1987 he led the Pacific Coast League in earned run average, shutouts, strikeouts and innings pitched. His face told me nothing except that he was a lineal descendant of the Mayans—I had last seen the face on certain statues in the museum in Mexico City—and when I asked him a question he showed no glimmer of understanding. I realized that he was as helpless in my language as I was in his; though I once lived for a month in a small Spanish village, my instant vocabulary pertained mainly to the food we had to buy every day. Vicente Palacios and I were shut off from each other in all but one area. Baseball was our link.

Palacios appeared to have a good chance of going north with the Pirates at the end of spring training, unlike Mike York. Meanwhile, Mike LaValliere, who would be their catcher when and if they made the club, was deliberately getting to know more about them—catchers are hunters and gatherers of information. LaValliere was another Pirate I soon began to notice in the clubhouse, partly because he didn't look like a ballplayer. He was as squat as a construction worker, with a face to match. Unlike the boyish Bob Walk, he was pre-grizzled.

LaValliere said that he uses spring training to do extra work on blocking balls, catching fouls, fielding bunts and other such thankless catching tasks. "Of course, that's something every catcher has done and done and done," he said. "But if I feel rusty about something, such as throwing to second base, I'll stay after a game and work on it, or work on my footwork.

Whatever doesn't feel right, that's what I'll work on, rather than saying, 'Today I'll do this, tomorrow I'll do that.' During the season you've got limited time to practice those things. Ideally, you want to come out of spring training in just perfect shape, ready to go."

Perfect shape for a catcher is also a mental condition. "There's a tremendous amount of communication in the catcher's job," LaValliere said, "and it goes on all the time. Here in spring training I talk to my pitchers constantly—not just when we're out on the field but right here in the clubhouse. I want to see how my pitchers are feeling. I want to know what their thoughts are."

*

What impressed me about the Pirate players was the orderliness with which they went about their work. They always knew where they were supposed to be. They had the look of college students going back and forth between classes. When I mentioned this to Syd Thrift, he said, "One thing a player will sense in a hurry is whether you're organized or not. If you're not organized you're dead, because you waste a lot of time, and these kids don't want to waste time.

"Another thing I like about these players is that they don't want to hear stories. They want to hear things that can help them. Many people talk deprecatingly about this generation. They say, 'Oh, these young players!' I say, 'That's hogwash! These guys are *bright!* They don't care who's been in the Hall of Fame. They don't know that stuff. So why take the time to tell them?' "

I asked Thrift whether he thought it would be helpful on some level if the players *did* know that stuff.

"Of course I do," he said. "I think history and tradition are very important. But it's not *the* most important thing for them at this age. It's where they're gonna go, what they're gonna do. *They* want to make some history too."

CHAPTER 6

Jim Leyland's School

It didn't take me more than a few minutes of Pirate-watching to figure out who the manager was. Jim Leyland (pronounced *Lee*land) was one of those men who you instantly know are in charge. His authority was visible in his get-there-and-get-it-taken-care-of walk, audible in his deep voice, and enjoyable in his enjoyment of a job that called for different skills—instructional, administrative, personal and diplomatic—from one minute to the next. He gave the same quality of attention to fans who stopped him for an autograph as he did to players who stopped him for advice. Physically, he wasn't big. He had a wiry build and a lean and hungry face, accented by a mustache that carried echoes of law enforcement. At forty-three, he looked like a man who has made it to the top by long, hard work and has no intention of blowing it by changing his ways.

Leyland's career is a case study of all the managers who have arrived in baseball's most visible job cloaked in anonymity (Jim who? Sparky who?), having had little major league playing experience themselves, or none, or, in the case of Walter Alston, who managed the Dodgers for twenty-three years, the nearest to none that was mathematically possible. Lodged somewhere in the cortex of every Dodgers fan is the fact that Alston's major league career consisted of one at-bat. (He struck out.) But in their long provincial exile the Alstons and the Tommy Lasordas and the Leylands don't go unnoticed by other baseball men, and when their moment comes they tend to make the most of it. Alston took the Dodgers to the World Series seven times and finished second eight times.

Jim Leyland is a native of Ohio and a product of the Detroit Tigers organization. He broke in as a catcher with Cocoa in the Florida League in 1964 and spent the next five seasons with Jamestown, Rocky Mount, Montgomery and Lakeland, seldom playing more than sixty games a season and never batting higher than .243. In 1970 he became a coach with Montgomery and in 1971 he was offered his first managing job, with Bristol in the Appalachian Rookie League, at the age of twenty-six. "The only reason I took the job," he once recalled, "is because I didn't have anything else to do. I didn't have an education; I was single." It never occurred to him, he said, that he might be the next Casey Stengel. "Bristol was so far from the major leagues that I didn't even think about it. 'A' ball is a million miles away."

From that youthful start Leyland moved steadily upward in the next decade, managing Clinton in the Midwest League, Montgomery in the Southern League, Lakeland in the Florida State League, and Evansville in the American Association. His teams won three league championships, he was named manager of the year three times, and he made the playoffs in five of his last six seasons. In 1982 he reached the major leagues as third-base coach of the Chicago White Sox, staying there for four years until Syd Thrift hired him as manager of the reconstituted Pirates at the end of 1985. Thrift's radical surgery wouldn't make the team healthy for another two years, but Leyland quickly established his own credibility. In early 1988 *Sports Illustrated* called him "the best young manager in the game," and every article written about him used the same word: "respect." He had brought discipline to a club that was in disarray and had won the respect of his players for his fairness. I asked him whether spring training was a time for building morale.

"It's a tough time for that," he said. "You come in with forty-five to fifty-five players, and obviously twenty-five of them know they're not going to make the team. That covers everything from green rookies to guys who've had some Triple A and maybe even some major league experience and who have hopes of making the team—they get their heart broken—to your veteran player, where the decision is made that he's had it and you end up releasing him. So it's not an easy time for keeping the spirits up.

"On the other hand, you have the advantage of a loose atmosphere. Because it *is* spring training and the games don't count, you can get a little closer to the players, on a casual basis. You're correcting mistakes by just normal conversation, whereas during the season when you're losing games you may get upset and it may be different. So the climate is pretty informal. Yet the tone is always just a good old-fashioned hard day's work. It starts real early and it goes *real* late, because the manager and the coaches work from six-thirty or seven in the morning to seven-thirty in the evening, and some of us also spend time at home at night going over rosters and lineups and possibilities. Last week there was one period when we spent twenty-four out of thirty-six hours at the ballpark. That's a pretty long day and a half.''

We were sitting in the dugout watching an infield workout. Leyland had taken his cap off and was smoking a cigarette—his version of the nerve medicine that every manager keeps handy. His hair, seen without the cap that hides so many tonsorial losses in the world of sport, was mostly gone on top, some of it perhaps having been torn out when pitchers gave one walk too many in Bristol, Clinton, Montgomery, Lakeland and Evansville. His brown eyes were warm and direct—they were eyes that a player could trust—and he spoke with confidence and ease, knowing exactly what he believed, the sentences forming themselves in methodical order. I told him I thought what he was really running was a school.

"That's exactly how I try to operate it," he said. "I gear my camp for the rawest rookie. We start from scratch and teach all the basic fundamentals, even though we've got quite a few players who have had major league experience, because one thing every organization takes pride in is, you don't want a player to go somewhere else and say, 'I've never heard that before.' We have one big meeting at the start of spring training with the general manager and all our minor league managers and coaches. We do an evaluation sheet on every player: his pluses and minuses, what he needs to work on in spring training, reports from the manager he played for the previous year. Then we go over each and every fundamental that we're going to teach and discuss how we're going to teach it, so that when we get out on the field there's no confusion about what we believe.

"One big change, of course, is that players come to a major league camp at a much younger age. We have players here who—if this was ten years ago—would still be in the minor leagues getting developed. It used to be nothing unusual to get a guy in spring training who had spent four years in Triple A ball and was coming to his first major league camp. Today kids play one or two years in the minors, or maybe just half a season, and then they're here. That's why there's much more teaching going on now than ever before."

Leyland has been so praised as a teacher of young players that I asked him if that was a talent that he thought he had a special aptitude for. "I'd like to think I could manage a veteran club or a rookie club," he said. "It really doesn't make any difference to me. In terms of instruction, you probably get better results from a younger club, because it would be pretty hard for a coach like Milt May to say anything to Wade Boggs about hitting, or for Ray Miller to say anything to Jack Morris about pitching. Not that the advice wouldn't be accepted; but your coaches have a better chance of conversing with the younger players who haven't already had a lot of success at the higher levels."

Listening to Leyland, I felt that he was a total realist—a man who saw the facts clearly and without sentiment. He was not a manager who would indulge in "if onlys" if his team lost a close game. Preparation was at the heart of his character: you do your best with what you're given.

"People have a tendency to say, 'Well, you've got a young club and you did a great job,'" Leyland went on. "But a guy like Dave Johnson did a great job with the Mets. It's true that with superstars you probably have a better chance to win, but that doesn't mean it's any easier. It's just as tough and maybe tougher to manage superstars than it is to manage a young club. Young players are still trying to earn their way, so they're going to be receptive. Veteran players sometimes aren't—and rightfully so; I don't have any problem with it. But a manager who wins with four or five superstars deserves just as much credit as someone with a young club. There are valid points for all managers. *Any*body who's managing in the big leagues today has his hands full."

One reason modern managers have their hands full, I thought, might be all that modern money. Wouldn't a player secure in a long-term multimillion-dollar contract, coddled by media celebrity, better known and better paid than his manager, be occasionally lulled into giving him less than full exertion?

"I sincerely believe that the money has nothing to do with it," Leyland said. "I give the players much more credit than that. Anyone can have a bad year, and when that happens everybody says, 'Well, he's got a big contract now and he doesn't care, so he had a bad year.' The players I've seen making the big money may not have been the most pleasant people to get along with in the clubhouse or out on the field, but every one of those guys had one thing in common: they busted their ass when the game started. All of us are too quick to generalize. I've seen guys who make big money occasionally dog it, but I've also seen guys who are making the minimum do the same thing. Sometimes you see a given day when a guy maybe can't run as hard as he did yesterday. But hell, nobody feels the same every day when they go to work—I know *I* come in some days and I'm not as peppy as I am some other days—and the sad part of our business is, if you're a fan and that's the game you happen to go to, that's the impression you may have gotten. But the players I've seen play hard. Guys like Tim Raines bust their butt."

*

Almost half of the players in the Pirates camp were black or Hispanic. They ranged from such regulars as Barry Bonds, Bobby Bonilla and R. J. Reynolds to rookies not long out of the Caribbean countries, knocking on baseball's biggest house of opportunity. One such opening on the Pirates was the position of shortstop, which was still unfilled. Two of the players competing for the job were from the Dominican Republic—Rafael Belliard and Felix Fermin—and the third, Al Pedrique, was from Venezuela. I asked Jim Leyland whether this contingent of players created any unusual situations in spring training.

"There are two things I think about in connection with the Latin players," he said. "One is that you have to be careful how you judge them in the spring, because sometimes they've been playing winter ball all year and they're fresh. They come to spring training and they just played a week ago in the Caribbean, whereas the guys from the North haven't been playing at all. The Latin players are hitting the hell out of the ball and you think, 'Holy Christ, this guy looks outstanding,' and then all of a sudden in June some of the other players start to catch up. So you can be fooled on your judgment. It's a really interesting scenario.

"But the big thing I think about is the language barrier. I never appreciated it until I managed in Venezuela one winter, and I've tried to stay on top of the situation ever since. I gained a lot of respect for the Latin players as a result of that experience. Not that I didn't respect them before, but I just didn't understand. I took it for granted that the Latin players on teams I managed here in the States knew what I was talking about. Some of them didn't. It never dawned on me until I got down to Venezuela and somebody gave me a clipboard with all these Spanish sayings on it, and I'm managing the team and *I'm* lost, and I go to a restaurant and I can order fish and one other thing and I don't know *what* I'm doing. You really learn to appreciate those poor kids coming here from one of those countries. There's so much that they just don't understand.

"So I try to make it a point that they *do* understand. We have a Spanish-speaking coach with us in spring training, Pablo Cruz, and that helps, because you never know when you're being misinterpreted. Hell, it could even get to the point where one of those guys thinks you told him something that you didn't tell him, or didn't tell him something that you did. You've got to be careful about that, because they're in a strange place. I really admire them for being able to come up here and adjust."

*

To be manager of the Pittsburgh Pirates is to be, if not an honorary citizen of Bradenton, at least an adopted son. The manager is the shepherd who brings the flock that renews the city's pride and prosperity every February,

generating the events that will make Bradenton a dateline held
in affection wherever baseball fans can buy a newspaper. He is
the person we most want to see at the ballpark. Leadership,
whatever the enterprise, is endlessly interesting, and if a
manager at a spring training camp happens to chat with us for
even a moment we remember it for the rest of our lives
("I was talking with Sparky Anderson once and he told
me . . .").

Jim Leyland was a fairly new son of Bradenton, but he came
from a long and colorful lineage—one that includes such men
as Frank Frisch, who managed the rowdy St. Louis Cardinals
in the early 1930s; Casey Stengel of the Boston Bees; "Birdie"
Tebbetts of the Milwaukee Braves; Ed Lopat of the Kansas
City A's, and the Pirates' last manager, Chuck Tanner, who
ran the club for nine years and gave Pittsburgh—and
Bradenton—their 1979 world championship. Tanner would be
a hard model to follow; he personified the kind of fatherly
stability that gets a man elected head of the chamber of
commerce in every Midwestern town. Reading old issues of
the *Bradenton Herald,* I was struck by how often Tanner turned
up at a Kiwanis Club breakfast or a Boosters Club barbecue or
some other local function.

Leyland was of a more feisty metabolism—the perfect
symbol of his scrappy young club, just as Tanner reflected the
aging Bucs of the old regime. Leyland was also immensely busy.
If it was true that all major league managers today have their
hands full, that was because baseball is a more complex business
every year, its financial stakes higher, its equilibrium shakier.
Some of the most vexing social issues of the day—drug testing
of athletes, violence in the stands—are being played out in the

boardrooms and locker rooms of the national pastime. Was there still time for the civilities between town and team that once gave spring training its distinctively American friendliness?

"I certainly feel that that's one of my responsibilities," Leyland said, "and I enjoy it. I go to different functions in Bradenton and talk about the club. I also enjoy talking to the people who come out to watch us play. A lot of them are snowbirds who have moved down here to Florida and who get caught up in the game because they love it. They're older folks, and it keeps them going. Getting an autograph is less of a problem—the players are so close, and they're apt to be more congenial because they're not suffering through a slump. The season's not on the line; it's not blue-chip time. Of course, this ballpark has a lot to do with it—it's got a warmth that you're not going to find in the new spring training facilities that are being built. Another thing I like about spring training is that the American League fans get a chance to see us, and our fans get a chance to see the American League teams. I have friends from my home in Ohio who come down every spring, and of course they stop and see me, but they also go around to just about every other camp. They see a different game somewhere every day."

Leyland's ultimate civic relationship, of course, is not with Bradenton but with Pittsburgh. His team and its city seemed to me to be well matched.

"Right now the Pirates are an example of what baseball is all about," he said. "We're developing a relationship with our fans and we're doing it by hard work. Pittsburgh is very much a workingman's city, and we're a perfect club for that city, because we've got a bunch of hungry players; they get their

CHAPTER 7

The Biggest Change

One of the fixed stars in the firmament of my boyhood as a Pirates follower was the presence in right and center field of Paul and Lloyd Waner, or "Big Poison" and "Little Poison," as they were called, in homage to their fearsome batting skills. They seemed to have been there forever. But except for a freakish turn of events at Pittsburgh's spring training camp in 1927, Lloyd would have taken longer to join his older brother in the lineup. I often thought of that incident when I was at the Pirates' camp in 1988. Nothing could dramatize more vividly what has been the single biggest change in spring training in all the decades since.

The story is told by Paul Waner in *The Glory of Their Times*, Lawrence S. Ritter's wonderful oral history of the early days of baseball. Waner recalls that during his rookie year with the Pirates in 1926 he told the club president, Barney Dreyfuss, that he had a younger brother back in Oklahoma who was even better than he was. Lloyd was duly signed to a contract and sent to Columbia, Pittsburgh's farm team in the Sally

League. The following year, Paul explains, "the Pirates took Lloyd along to spring training, mostly just to look at him a little closer. They never thought he could possibly make the team, because Lloyd only weighed about 130 pounds then. He was only twenty years old and was even smaller than me.

"Our outfield that season was supposed to be Kiki Cuyler, Clyde Barnhart and myself. But Barnhart reported for that spring training weighing about 260 or 270 pounds. He was just a butterball. They took him and did everything they could think of to get his weight down. They gave him steam baths, and exercised him, and ran him, and ran him, and ran him. Well, they got the weight off, all right, but as a result the poor fellow was so weak he could hardly lift a bat.

"So on the trip back to Pittsburgh from spring training, Donie Bush came to me and said, 'Paul, I'm putting your little brother out there in left field, and he's going to open the season for us.'

" 'Well, you won't regret it,' I said. 'Lloyd will do the job in first-rate style.' "

The promise was, if anything, understated. Lloyd got 223 hits that year and batted .355. Paul got 237 hits and batted .380. Of those 460 fraternal hits, only eleven were home runs; the rest, Paul says, were "mostly line drives: singles, doubles and a lot of triples, because both of us were very fast." Propelled by such big and little poison, the Pirates won the pennant, though Paul denies that it was a family accomplishment, pointing out that Pie Traynor hit .342 that season in addition to being, defensively, "the greatest third baseman who ever lived."

That was the first of fourteen summers in which Paul and

Lloyd Waner formed two-thirds of the Pirate outfield, and when they were traded to other clubs after the 1940 season they each played five more years, Paul finally amassing 3,100 hits and Lloyd 2,500. Their combined career total of 5,600 major league hits exceeds by almost 1,000 the number achieved by all five Delehanty brothers, and by more than 500 the number achieved by the three DiMaggios. As for Clyde Barnhart, his entry in *The Baseball Encyclopedia* ends in 1928, just one year after he turned up for spring training at butterball weight.

His is a fate that few players today would risk—too much money is at stake. That never used to be a factor. Until ten or fifteen years ago the first purpose of spring training was for ballplayers to get back in condition. One reason they were in poor shape was that they had to take other jobs when the season ended. They sold real estate or had car dealerships and gave no thought to exercise when 5 P.M. arrived, preferring, like most American working males, to wash down the tensions and boredoms of the day with a few beers. Quite a few evenings also got spent on the banquet circuit, where summertime exploits were rewarded with wintertime celebrity and high-cholesterol meals. As a result, spring training found most ballplayers looking less than trim. "My first priority down here," they would tell the hometown sportswriters, "is to get myself down to playing weight." Poundage figured remarkably often in the dispatches that the writers wrote for the folks back home.

Two social revolutions have changed all that. Big money now dominates American sport, and fitness has become a national religion. Today a major league player earns enough money in seven months of baseball to support himself and his family for twelve months of the year; he doesn't need to take a second job. And because his body is the source of his present and future income, he sees it as an investment to be protected. Now what he tells the press when he arrives in Florida is, "I've been doing weights all winter." The writers duly note his thickened deltoids and predict that he'll hit twenty points higher.

"When I played," Jim Leyland told me, "you ate Ma's cooking during the off season and you drank milk shakes or beer, whichever was your choice, and you came to spring training with a ten-pound winter beer belly on, and you ran about thirty sprints and you sweated with a sweat jacket and you got yourself in condition. Now the players do Nautilus all winter, they play racquetball, they swim, they exercise, and they come to spring training looking like Tarzan. It's still not exactly a baseball shape, but it's a much better and stronger shape than it used to be. This year there may have been two or three players at the most who came in here overweight."

*

Kent Biggerstaff, the Pirates' trainer, who has been with the club since 1982, is a short, forty-one-year-old man with amused eyes and a relaxed manner; muscles wouldn't tighten in his presence. Like Leyland, he came to the major leagues trailing a long itinerary of minor league posts, starting with Marion, Virginia, in the Appalachian League club and winding through Memphis in the Texas League, Tidewater in the International League, Holyoke in the Eastern League, and Vancouver and Portland in the Pacific Coast League. I found him in the training room in the clubhouse at McKechnie Field, standing next to a machine that looked as if it could make a computer printout of world rainfall and population trends. No old-fashioned smells of unguents and ointments defiled the high-tech air.

"When I broke in as a trainer at Marion in 1967," he said, "there was very little equipment at the spring training camp. You just opened the doors and a hundred and seventy people came in. The only ones who did any real conditioning were guys who had been injured and were trying to get rehabilitated. Today if a player came to spring training with that attitude he'd end up not making the club."

The same casual attitude was held by the management. Twenty years ago a baseball club said goodbye to its players in October and didn't much care what they did. Now it keeps a stern parental eye on them. "At the end of the season," Biggerstaff said, "we give each player an individualized program for the winter. If someone was injured we examine him and prescribe a program to get him back to full health. I advise every player to throw at least three times a week—that prevents a lot of shoulder adhesions. We preface all our work with a talk about how well you can do financially in baseball today if you're fit. That's a big motivator. I also point out that in the short run you may not notice the effects of harmful things you're doing, but in the long run they'll shorten your career. The result is that players take their winter exercise very seriously. Many of them add rooms to their homes so they can install Nautilus machines, or free weights, or Universal—whatever they prefer. They also use local facilities like the high school gym."

When the Pirate players arrive for spring training they get a complete physical, including a blood test, which may show that they need dietary supplements. They also get examined on the Cybex machine, which tests all the major joints and makes a printout of muscle strength. "That enables us to detect players who are injury prone," Biggerstaff said, "and to work on strengthening that specific weakness. For players who don't have a deficit, the chart gives us a baseline in case anything *does* happen to them." He gave the Cybex an admiring pat. "We also refamiliarize them with the sun when they arrive down here. Many of them are pale from spending the winter up North, and there's a real danger of dehydration."

Around us in the room, players were using weight-lifting devices, soaking their limbs in whirlpool baths and otherwise delivering themselves over to science. I asked Biggerstaff what the training room would have looked like twenty years ago.

"It would look just the way it looks now," he said, "except that it would be empty. Maybe there'd be a whirlpool bath. Mostly what you'd find was horse liniments—I remember one that was called Sloan's horse liniment. The liniments they make today probably use the same base, but they smell better and have different names. Actually, most of the work that's done in a training room is still hands-on work. We'll do more massage in a day of spring training than a football team will do in a week." He was referring to himself and his assistant trainer, David Tumbas.

"There's a lot of stiffness in spring training," Biggerstaff said. "The players are suddenly running on grass after a winter of running on hard floors, and they've got a lot of aches and pains in their legs. We want to help every one of them to feel fit and to get well if they're hurt. In baseball, what most people consider a minor injury is often a major one. Football players play with broken bones, but you can't play baseball with a jammed finger."

Haste in spring training is one of the villains. "Many players try to overimpress somebody too soon—especially rookies and free agents," Biggerstaff said. "They're trying to make the team right from the start. You see them throwing hard sooner than they should, instead of taking a few weeks to get ready for the exhibition games, and they get themselves in shoulder-threatening and career-threatening situations. People often wonder why there are so many more torn rotator cuff injuries today than there used to be. Probably there are no more than there ever were, but in the old days people would say, 'Hey, the guy got a dead arm.' Today there's a tremendous improvement in education and in diagnostic methods and treatment. With the evolution of arthroscopic surgery you can look inside a knee or an arm and see what the problem is. That takes all the guesswork away. Then you can go in and clean it out. I find that very satisfying."

*

One person who needed no evangelizing on this subject is Syd Thrift. If today's knowledge had existed a generation ago, he might be remembered as a left-handed pitcher for the Yankees. When Thrift went to the Yankees' instructional school in 1950 he was both a pitcher and a first baseman. "Every day I'd switch from one thing to the other," he recalled, "because they couldn't decide what to do with me.

I was a left-handed hitter, and I suppose they had hopes of me hitting at Yankee Stadium."

The decision was made that summer when Thrift was sent to Amsterdam in the Canadian-American League. His manager was Mayo Smith, who subsequently managed in the major leagues for nine years with the Phillies, the Reds and the Tigers. "Mayo decided I was a pitcher," Thrift said, "so that's what I was, and I got off to a great start—I won three or four games real quick. But then I began to be aggravated with nagging injuries. I had never been injured before, and I didn't know how to live with it. The training and medical facilities weren't what they are today. I'm sure those things I suffered with for a couple of months could have been cleaned up if I had just been given some rest. I learned a lot from that experience—it taught me the value of having knowledgeable people as trainers."

Released by the Yankees, Thrift went into the army for two years in 1951. He was active in army baseball as a player and as a playing manager, often finding himself in illustrious company; he remembers the day at Fort Eustis, Virginia, in 1952, when Willie Mays turned up. When Thrift got out, he went to spring training with the Oakland Oaks. "I was going along fine," he recalled, "when one day all of a sudden I had a real problem with my left shoulder, which, of course, was my pitching arm. I didn't want to talk about it because I was trying to hide it, like most players—I thought maybe it was a spring training thing and it would go away. It never did go away. Finally George Bamberger, who was rooming next to me, insisted on me going to the trainer. The trainer worked on me for half an hour, working on my right shoulder. I didn't know he wasn't supposed to do that, because I had never had a trainer really work on me before, and George came in and asked why he was working on my *right* shoulder. That's how green I was.''

The Oaks gave up on him, and Thrift was about to go home when he got a call from a club in Williamsburgh, Florida. "A guy I had played with knew that the team needed a left-handed hitter," he said, "and he told the manager about me. So I went there to be a hitter because I couldn't throw. I really couldn't throw. A lot of times it hurt me even to take the infield. But I stuck it out to probably the middle of August. Finally I said, 'The heck with this—it's just too much of an ordeal.' So that ended my professional playing career—not a very long one, but a lot of miles.''

The pain in Thrift's arm has stayed with him ever since—not as a pain but as information. "There's no such thing as a little sore arm," he says. "If it's sore there's something wrong with it.''

CHAPTER *8*

Hitting

The sound of the bat is the music of spring training. It runs like a fugue through the lives of the players and the fans, brightening the day with memories and associations. No other sound is quite like it, and no word quite describes it. To speak of the "crack" of the bat doesn't catch the music—the high-pitched resonance, the suggestion of an echo. But it does catch the energy of the moment: a ball literally springing off wood. In the physics of baseball this is the central collision, the origin of life.

At McKechnie Field I was struck by how early in the morning the music began and how late it went on. What it conveyed was: there's not a minute to lose. At every exhibition game, right after the final out, before the fans had even begun to leave, the batting cage was wheeled out to home plate so that the players could get back to the business of getting in more licks. Nobody had to tell them, as so many people kept reminding me, that hitters have a failure rate of 70 percent. Up against such arithmetic, they are on an eternal quest to find an edge, however slight, in their classic duel with the pitcher, and it begins as soon as they arrive at spring training. Summer's reflexes have been dulled by fall and winter: the eye is a little off, the wrists are a little slow, the rhythms a little jerky. Only one process will put things right—hitting ball after ball after ball, rediscovering how pitches arrive at the plate in all their velocities and curves and dips, learning to relax, learning to *believe*.

The sound of the bat at McKechnie Field came not only from home plate, where hitters were hitting against real pitchers. It also came from a cage near the clubhouse, where a machine fired endless strikes at an endless procession of Pirates. Taking their turn according to a schedule that seemed to be posted only in their heads, the players stepped into the cage and swung ferociously at the robot's fastball, working at little corrections in their stance or in their hands or in the position of the bat. It was drill, pure and simple, and they went at it with intense concentration.

Supervising all this physical and diagnostic work was the Pirates' hitting coach, Milt May. The son of "Pinky" May, an infielder with the Phillies from 1939 to 1943, Milt May is a boyish-looking man of thirty-seven with a round and open face, distinguishable from his pupils only because the team is so young. A catcher in his own playing days, May broke in with the Pirates in 1970 and spent fourteen seasons in the majors, including stints with the Astros, Tigers, White Sox and Giants. Reacquired by Pittsburgh in 1983, he quit after the 1984 season and subsequently became the club's advance scout and also a catching and hitting instructor in its minor league system. He was now in his second year as the Pirates' hitting coach.

"Hitting is one area where you can't come up with a machine," May told me one day before a game with the Phillies. "There's no substitute for individual work. Hitting is the toughest thing in baseball; Ted Williams said that if you can do it three times out of ten and be considered great it must be tough. When all is said and done, baseball comes down to hitting a ball, throwing a ball, and catching a ball, and the guy who's good at hitting is the guy whose picture you want on a card."

Because of the new attention to fitness, May said, he can do much more teaching than would have been possible twenty years ago, when he would have largely lost three weeks while the players limbered up. "My father was an exception," he said. "He had been throwing bales of hay around all winter on our farm in Indiana." Again, rural America was heard from as a current in my story. "Today I can begin to work with the players on the mechanics of hitting immediately. You can start right out of the chute."

Even such a start doesn't put the hitter ahead. "It's harder to be a good hitter today than it's ever been before," May said. "There are three reasons for that. First, pitching has become a far more specialized skill. Pitchers nowadays are trained to be either starters or long relievers or stoppers. When I came up in 1968, relief pitchers were pitchers who weren't good enough to start. Now they're some of the biggest stars in the game." He pointed to Steve Bedrosian, the Phillies' formidable stopper, who was standing next to the visitors' dugout. "A team will often say, 'Let's try to get a big lead so we won't have to face a Bedrosian, or a Gossage, or a Righetti.' The result of these changes is that a hitter often has only two at-bats against the starting pitcher. Just when he begins to figure him out they bring in a long reliever, who may have a side-arm specialty or some other tricky delivery, and then for his final at-bat they bring in the stopper."

The second reason why hitting is harder is that defensive play is better. "Managers today are putting more emphasis on using infielders who have range," May said, "because with an artificial surface in so many parks, the ball gets through the infield faster. Defense has become critical."

The third reason is that pitchers are throwing a greater assortment of pitches. "For instance," May said, "most everybody now throws a fork ball. It's thrown with the same arm action as a fastball, but it's an off-speed pitch, so it's difficult to pick up. I'm not saying that guys are throwing *better* today; they're just throwing more kinds of pitches. Still, a good hitter will always hit well. Those great old-timers, if they played today, would do well because they would adjust to the conditions."

John Cangelosi, a reserve Pirate outfielder, came over to ask May if there was any time when he could get in some extra hitting.

"How about after the game today?" May suggested.

"O.K.," Cangelosi said.

"Good," May said. "I'll see you there."

I asked May about the rhythm of spring training—the successive stages that a hitter needs to get himself ready. "The pitchers and the catchers arrive at Pirate City first, before anybody else," he explained. "That's because before you can play baseball you have to have pitchers who are ready to pitch. The pitching machine isn't adequate because it doesn't provide a real simulated pitch—it has no arm or body motion. It's useful for the first few weeks because the first thing a batter has to do in spring training is to get his hands tough, and get his hands strong, and get his swing in rhythm, and get used to seeing the ball, and you can't accomplish that against a real pitcher because the pitcher's arm wears out. The machine's arm doesn't. But *then* you have to bat against real pitchers.

"At that stage you're working on seeing the ball real well. You're working on mechanics—you're not interested in results. Sure, we all like base hits, but that's not as important as getting your mechanics right; when your timing is gone, nothing else matters. Those mechanics will differ from one player to another—it depends on what each person needs. You might have a guy who's having a hard time going the other way—hitting to the opposite field. So you work on that. Or he's not a good bunter. Or he swings at a lot of bad pitches, so you get him to learn to take pitches. Those are the things you work on in spring training. That's what you're here for, and you've got six weeks to do it."

Six weeks was what everybody got—a fixed unit of time. Yet there were probably twenty-six different ways of breaking it down; no two major league clubs had the same goals and values.

"Jim Leyland has the most organized spring training of any camp I've ever been to," May said. "It makes the best use of time. That's important to any club, but with a young club like this one, which has so much to learn, it's critical. We get on the field at nine-thirty, and Jim stretches the whole ball club. At ten we practice a particular fundamental that he wants to work on that day. It might be cutoffs and relays, or maybe

defense against the double steal, or offense of the double steal—
plays that involve the whole team. After that we break into
small groups—the infielders might work on double plays, the
catchers on blocking the ball, the pitchers on pickoff moves or
covering first base, and the hitters on their mechanics. We do
those things every day for two weeks at Pirate City, and then
when we move to McKechnie Field for our schedule of exhibition games we spend the mornings fine-tuning what we've been
working on."

The sentence summoned back one of my oldest images of
spring training. The time is midsummer, the moment a crucial
one in the pennant race. Two teams are locked in a late-inning
struggle, and one of them makes a complex and seemingly
effortless defensive play that saves the game. Afterward, the
manager tells the press, "We worked on that all spring." At
such moments I always visualized a field somewhere in Florida
and a squad of players being put through numbingly repetitious
drills. Did they ever have any idea that their dreary labors in
March would have such a satisfying payoff in August?

*

Out on the field, the Phillies finished batting
practice. The daunting Bedrosian was no longer anywhere in
sight. Soon enough, if not this afternoon, then on some other
afternoon, he would materialize from the bullpen late in the
game to try to smoke the ball past May's hitters.

Jim Leyland stopped to ask May a question, and the two of
them went into the dugout and studied some charts. Paperwork, I had noticed, is almost as basic to the game as the ball

and bat; somewhere behind every human decision on the field
is a piece of writing or a set of figures. Sid Bream, the Pirate
first baseman, came over to see me; I had asked him earlier if I
could talk to him, but he had a date with a pitching machine.
Bream was one of the Pirates I most enjoyed watching. A tall,
thin, twenty-seven-year-old man with a thin face, black hair
and genial blue eyes, he has the loose-jointed motions of a
classic southpaw or of Ray Bolger's Straw Man in *The Wizard
of Oz*. I liked his relaxed and graceful style around first base and
his equally relaxed left-handed swing, which, in his two seasons
as a Pirate regular, has delivered a surprising number of doubles
and home runs. His personality was equally easygoing.

"Spring training for me is a time to work on things I failed
to do the year before," Bream said. "If I had trouble picking
up grounders backhanded I'll work on that, or I might ask the
coaches to give me extra time picking throws out of the dirt.
But this year I have one major objective, and it's in hitting. I'm
trying to develop a consistent stance at the plate, so I can go
up there every time and know what I'm supposed to be doing—
where my hands are supposed to be, where my feet are
supposed to be—and can take that stance through the whole
season. I want to stop making adjustments after the season
starts.

"They always say you have to make an adjustment at least
every at-bat. Some people say you have to make an adjustment
on every pitch. But those should be minor adjustments. In the
past I've been making major adjustments—for instance, when
I'm in a slump—and when you do that and then try to get back
to where you used to be, you lose what was in your mind. So
what I'm trying to do in spring training is to establish a norm
for my swing that I can hold in my head all season long."

When Milt May finished talking with Leyland, I asked him whether the art of hitting could be reduced to a set of principles.

"It definitely can," he said. "There are certain absolutes for every hitter. Number one is, you must see the ball. The best hitters see the ball more consistently than other hitters—and I mean they see it from the time it leaves the pitcher's hand. You can't just pick it up halfway to the plate.

"Two is, you must have good plate coverage. When your front foot hits the ground, your bat must be able to reach every part of the plate.

"Three: At that same point your bat has to be in a strong position—that is, it has to be back.

"Four: You have to keep your head down through contact. You have to keep looking down and keep your eye on the ball.

"Finally, you must hit through the ball." He stated the principle with such certainty that I wanted to be sure I knew what he meant. "I mean," he said, "that you must stay on the plane of the ball." He went and got a bat and took a left-handed swing, keeping his bat level. "That way," he said, "you're on the plane of the ball longer."

I had no trouble believing that he had hit through the ball. Where it went I could only imagine.

CHAPTER *9*

Running

All batters turn at some point into baserunners, whereupon they are confronted with the game's fundamental problem: how to get home. A runner's ability to move himself safely around the bases is often the difference between victory and defeat, and at spring training the Pirates spent many hours in the practice of that complicated art. A typical class was one I saw Jim Leyland conducting on what he called "situation hitting." It looked more like situation running.

"It's where you have different runners on different bases," Leyland explained, "and you teach them how to advance on a ball hit behind them, how to hold up on a ball hit in front of them, how to work the hit-and-run and the suicide squeeze—all the different things that actually happen in a game. You're saying, 'Now, the first thing you're going to do is, you're going to find out where the outfielders are playing. The next thing you're going to think about is, there's nobody out, so if the ball is hit in front of you—to the shortstop or the third baseman—you've got to hold. If the ball's hit behind you to the second baseman you've got to react and go.' What you're really teaching them is how to read the ball off the bat. That means you follow the pitch all the way to the plate, and you look into the strike zone, and you watch the hitter swing the bat through the strike zone, and wherever he hits it you're reading the ball to find out if you can advance. It's a matter of trying to improve the runners' instincts. It's also a very good drill for the hitters—especially on contact plays such as the hit-and-run. I like the drill because it uses hitters and runners and fielders all at the same time, so you kill three birds with one stone."

Out on the diamond, multiples of birds were being killed. Leyland stationed himself near second base, instructing runners who had reached first base by running out their last swing at bat. "It's easy to get lazy and not practice reading the ball off the bat," Leyland told me later. "For example, the custom in batting practice is that after you take your last swing you run around the bases. However, you don't really concentrate—you just run around the bases because that's what everybody has done for fifty years. But there's a purpose to that drill. After you take your last swing you're supposed to stop at first base, and when the next batter comes up you take your lead, and when he bunts you react: if the ball's up in the air you can't go; if it's on the ground you make sure it's on the ground and *then* you react. Just reading things.

"Naturally, pitching and catching and hitting are the most important skills in baseball, but it's these little basic things"—he pointed to a runner making a turn at second base—"that often mean the difference between winning the close games and not winning them. That's why you practice them intensively down here in spring training. You program them into the player's mind. You make it so repetitious that it becomes a habit. If a runner is on second base with nobody out he should *know* he can't run on a ball that's hit in front of him. But sometimes, if he's not concentrating, he runs. Whereas if a player is programmed, he normally will not and should not make that mistake."

The person most responsible for getting Pirate players home is third-base coach Gene Lamont. Lamont, who is forty-one, was hired in the fall of 1985, one day after Leyland was named manager; obviously the new regime knew who it wanted as its traffic director. A catcher in his thirteen-year career with the Detroit organization, Lamont appeared in only eighty-seven games for the parent Tigers, spending the rest of his playing days in Daytona Beach, Statesville, Rocky Mount, Montgomery, Toledo, Richmond and Evansville. Next he was a manager for eight years—at Fort Myers, Jacksonville and Omaha—in the farm system of the Kansas City Royals. Ten members of the Royals' 1985 world champion club played for Lamont at some point in their rise to glory.

A gentle and scholarly-looking man, Lamont has none of the nervous energy that I associate with third-base coaches. Even before the advent of television any fan could see with his naked eye that the man at third is a tireless transmitter of information, his hands fluttering with signals to his hitters and runners and hit-and-runners. TV's lens has only magnified his role as the game's activating agent. All is in abeyance as the batter peers down the third-base line to get his orders. Not until he understands the coded language of his guru can the game proceed. How the coach gets *his* orders from the manager is the mystery behind the mystery.

"In spring training, basically I talk to the players about the things that I as the third-base coach want them to do," Lamont told me. He had just come in from the coach's box at third—his rectangular kingdom. "This spring, for instance, we've stressed getting a walking lead at third base, trying to score on balls that are hit to the infield. Last year we just weren't very good at that, so we're working hard on the proper technique. Since I'm the one who's going to be down here at third with them during a game, I feel a strong responsibility for making sure they're executing it as it was taught. We've also been talking about the different ways a man on second base can get to third without the ball being hit to the right side. I have the advantage of being able to see that situation a little better from over here at third base."

Earlier I had noticed Lamont holding workshops in the giving and receiving of signs. Amid so much attention to the body, it was a reminder that the brain is a big component of the game and also needs a spring tune-up. More runs are scored by opportunism than by brawn—by the ability of batters and runners to move themselves and each other around the bases by processing signs from the third-base coach. So Byzantine are these signals—so elaborate a pantomime of truth and deception—that I often marvel that the system works as well as it does, and I asked Lamont how these intellectual arts are imparted.

"We do it a little differently from when I was with other clubs," he said. "We have kind of a class—we take about ten guys and go over the signs together. I try to stress to them, 'This is not to embarrass you, but I absolutely must get an idea of who gets signs well.' If they're not good at it you need to take them aside and spend a little extra time with them. But what you really have to do is watch them during a game to see if they're catching the signs. Sometimes I'll say, 'Hey, you give *me* the bunt sign,' and see if they can do it. Often they know the sign but can't give it to someone else. That's a pretty good indication that they really don't understand; I can usually tell.

"Another problem is that they *act* different after you give them a sign, especially batters. They tense up, and I have to impress on them, 'When I give you the hit-and-run sign you have to behave the same. You can't give it away by looking down at the runner on first base, or things like that.' We've been pretty good with our signs, but I definitely have to find out who can't get them, because we're not a team that's going to overpower other teams. We have to do the little things to get runs, and we have to do them right. We can't miss a hit-and-run and get a guy thrown out at second base."

Lamont struck me as a modest man and therefore an unlikely mummer in the coach's box. I couldn't picture him making all those motions that third-base coaches revel in, successively touching different parts of their uniform or their body in a feverish display of real and false information.

"I'd say probably eighty percent of those motions are no sign at all," Lamont said. "I personally don't give as many signs as most coaches do. I just don't think it's necessary. There are any number of times when a sign that's already been given is still on, and everybody in the ballpark knows it's still on. I don't see any reason to give it again—it might mess things up, and it could even prolong the game. If there's a situation where there's no way there could be something on, I don't give any sign at all."

CHAPTER *10*

A Day at the Ballpark

At 9:30 A.M., Jack Stuhltrager, president of the Bradenton Pirates Boosters, arrives at McKechnie Field and unlocks a small cinder-block room under the grandstand. Its shelves are stacked with copies of the 1988 Pirates program that the Boosters will sell at today's game against the Blue Jays and with the seat cushions they will rent to fans who anticipate needing relief from McKechnie's wooden seats before the afternoon is over.

The Boosters have more than a vendors' interest in the forty-page program. They also produced it, soliciting the many pages of advertisements taken by Bradenton businesses, banks, realtors, restaurants, motels, fruit farms, churches, fraternal organizations, retirement homes and funeral homes. Proceeds from the sale of the programs and from the rental of the seat cushions go into the renovation and maintenance of McKechnie Field. "Every year we walk around the field and see what needs to be done," says vice-president Bob Johnson. So far the Boosters have raised $110,000 for such capital needs. Among other improvements, the outfield is no longer the cow pasture that Whitey Herzog called it in 1979; the infield is smooth; the visitors' locker room is a fit place for a person to change clothes; two sets of bleachers, seating two thousand people, have been added (total capacity is around five thousand), and one section of the grandstand has been fitted with ramps to accommodate wheelchairs.

"I'm from Philadelphia, and I was a Phillies fan all my life," Jack Stuhltrager tells me. "But after I moved down here and retired, I went out to the ballpark one day to buy some tickets and I saw a sign saying they needed volunteer ushers. I figured, '*This* is my hometown. I should be a Pirates fan.' "

That was ten years ago. Today the Boosters have 272 members, all volunteers, who pay annual dues of five dollars for the privilege of working hard during the Pirates' month at McKechnie Field. Their president is one of the first to get there and last to leave. "By the time spring training is over," says Stuhltrager, who is sixty-seven, "it's beginning to seem like a job, and you think, 'I didn't retire for *that*.' But when fall rolls around we can't wait for it to start all over again."

By ten o'clock the room under the grandstand has begun to quicken with activity. Men and women, mostly in their fifties and sixties, drop in to get their assignment for the day from Jack Stuhltrager ("We're going to be needing two more ushers") or from Ken Carlson, the Boosters' secretary ("Can you do cushions today, Pat?"). They remind me of people getting ready for a church picnic. Somebody makes coffee. The talk is easy, the banter good-natured.

"Every December we hold a kaffeeklatsch for the Boosters out at Pirate City," Ken Carlson says. "We serve coffee and doughnuts, and one of the Pirate coaches like Milt May and a couple of players come and tell us about the off-season trades and the prospects for the year. In January we hold a luncheon at the Elks Club or at a restaurant downtown; that's attended by some other Pirate players and maybe the manager. Chuck Tanner was always a popular speaker at those events—he was an eternal optimist. Then after spring training starts we have an evening banquet at the American Legion Hall. Forty or fifty people from the Pirates are usually there: Jim Leyland, players, coaches, folks from the front office, and a lot of wives. It's a nice event."

Photographs of Boosters and ballplayers are tacked up all over the walls. Bob Johnson points to one that shows Ken Carlson throwing out the first ball at Three Rivers Stadium in Pittsburgh. "Every summer about sixty of us go up to Pittsburgh for three games," he says. "We pay our own way, and we take our wives, and usually we also have some widows along, and one of us throws out the first ball." Johnson, who was originally from Wisconsin, makes the junket every year. "We've been up there through the lean years—we're loyal fans through thick and thin," he says, "and the Pirates take good care of us. Sometimes they take us on boat trips. We've been up the Allegheny and up the Monongahela and down the Ohio."

"The wives use the opportunity to go shopping," Jack Stuhltrager adds. "One year they bought Gimbel's out."

It was Bob Johnson who had the idea of adapting one part of the stands for fans in wheelchairs. Many handicapped people now come to McKechnie Field to watch spring training games who never could have managed it before.

At eleven o'clock, several men and women who will be selling programs or renting cushions take their wares and leave. The gates are open, and fans are beginning to arrive to watch batting practice. All the Boosters wear a bright orange cap with a big "P" that can be spotted by anyone in need of help.

"This is our office only during games," Ken Carlson explains. "Our treasurer, Cheryl Brown, is married to Chuck Brown, who owns Brown's Funeral Home, and that's basically our headquarters. Even the embalmer will answer questions about the Boosters."

"That's a fun place," Jack Stuhltrager says.

*

This winter the Boosters have been cosponsoring an essay contest—150 words or less—on "What Baseball Means to Me" for kids of Little League age (ten and eleven), and the results are just in. Other sponsors and judges were the Manatee County Chamber of Commerce, the Department of Parks and Recreation, the Board of Education, the Pittsburgh Pirates, the Little League, and City Councilman Fred Reynolds. The chairman of the committee is Stephen Korcheck, president of Manatee Community College, who was a catcher with the Washington Senators in the 1950s.

First Prize went to Marcus Crow, a fourth grader in Mrs. Babson's class at Bayshore Elementary School. He wrote:

I have enjoyed baseball since I was three years old.
My dad and I spent a lot of time tossing a ball in our
backyard. I learned about sportsmanship too. Because he

cheered me on I didn't lose confidence in myself. Now I'm in Little League. My dad does a lot of cheering for my team.

People say that baseball is THE sport of America. I agree. I like to play it. I like to watch it. I like to read about it. I'm a real fan! I go to all the Pirates' games in Bradenton. All the Pirates have signed my cards!

Last year my team made it to the play offs. We lost in the World Series. Even though we were losers on the outside we were winners in our hearts. A lot of people play just to win but I play to have fun. That's what baseball means to me.

Working on a broader geographical scale, one of the runners-up, William Campbell, a fifth grader in Mrs. Russell's class at Palma Sola Elementary School, wrote:

A person in New York City can talk to a person in Los Angeles about baseball. A person in San Diego can talk to a person in Miami about baseball. That's one of the things that ties America together. To me, baseball means more than the American pastime. It is part of the American way of life. Anyone can play. It doesn't matter what size you are; big or small, short or tall, anyone can dream about being the next Willie Mays or Dale Murphy. I know I have that dream. The confidence I gain in baseball helps in everything I do. Every time I go up to bat, I feel like I am going to hit a home run. But if I don't, I know I can do it the next time, whether it's baseball or anything else I do.

Another runner-up, Keith Williams, a fourth grader in Mrs. Belcher's class at Oneco Elementary School, concluded his essay with this paragraph:

It's hard to lose. It's even harder if you win the wrong way. When you win wrong you feel bad. The wrong way is by cheating or being a show-off or bad-mouthing the other team. If I start that, Mom puts a stop to it real quick. She tells me it's only a game and somebody has to win. If one team wins, the other loses and it could have been ours just as easily.

*

Cap and Bev Waterman, a retired couple from upstate New York, run the ticket office at McKechnie Field, and when I drop in to see them around eleven-fifteen, they are almost too busy to talk. Cap is working the window and Bev is answering the phone. Every time I ask Bev a question, the phone rings. "It's worse than ever before," she says. "But better, of course. There's a much more positive attitude this year. People are beginning to see that we might have a ball team."

Many of the ticket buyers arriving at the window are parents or grandparents with children. Often, Bev says, they call the box office in advance. "They ask, 'Will the kids be able to get autographs, and what's the best time to do that?' We tell them that the gates open at eleven and that if they stand along the railing the players are out on the field taking batting practice and they'll usually come over and sign a baseball. Sometimes people ask, 'Who's pitching today?' When *we* used to come down to Florida on our vacation it was just to see a ballgame."

The questions that Cap gets at the window often pertain to spring training's other big attraction:

"Are the bleachers in the sun?"

"Yes, ma'am."

"Oh, wonderful!"

But it's not always wonderful. "Some of them have skin cancer and want to be sure they're *out* of the sun," Cap says. "Or maybe they were at the beach the day before and got sunburned."

This year the ballpark did a bigger mail order business than ever before. "We sent ticket information to thirty of the forty-eight continental United States," Bev says. "We get fans in every combination, from singles to groups of two hundred. Last week when the Phillies were here we had a 'Pennsylvania Club'—that's two hundred people who originally came to Bradenton from Pennsylvania and now live in one of the trailer camps. They always order tickets for a Phillies game. One year they sit on the Pirates' side and the next year they sit on the Phillies' side."

At the window, Cap is wrestling with a common problem—unexpected vacationers from up North. "We've got four tickets already," a woman is explaining, "but we've just heard from two old friends who are driving down from Ohio. Can you give us all seats together?" The people who come to the ticket window at McKechnie Field on any given morning are a group portrait of the spring training spectator population: retired men and women from the area; middle-aged couples from out of state who have timed their vacation to see their favorite teams and warm their bones; parents shepherding school-age kids who are on their own spring vacation; solitary fans making their rounds of as many camps as they can squeeze into a week—today Bradenton, tomorrow Lakeland, Thursday Kissimmee, Friday Vero Beach. The typical fan attends seven or eight games during the Grapefruit League's four-week exhibition schedule, according to a study commissioned in 1987 by the state Department of Commerce. The eighteen major league teams that train in Florida generate approximately $295 million in tourist income, or an average of $16.4 million each. Bradenton is above average: fans who come to McKechnie Field to watch the Pirates will spend almost $18.2 million in Manatee County for lodging, food, parking, souvenirs and other services. March is Florida's biggest tourist month.

"We never get to see a game," Bev tells me, "so the only thing we know about the Pirates is what we read in the paper." Her phone is giving her no rest—as soon as she finishes with one caller, another is on the line. She doesn't hurry any of them.

"Are you coming up Forty-one or Seventy-five, sir? O.K. Watch for Ninth Street West, and you're going to turn left. Just continue down Ninth Street, and it's about eight or nine blocks. You'll see us right there."

She hangs up. The phone rings again instantly.

"You're in Siesta Key?" Bev says. "You want the northern-most exit. It's going to be state road Sixty-four, and you'll be driving east. It's going to be three or four miles, and then you'll see . . ."

The pilgrims continue to call to ask directions to the shrine. "I suppose we could get a tape to provide this information," Bev says, "but it wouldn't be the same."

I ask her how she got so good at dealing with people.

"When we lived up North," she says, "I worked for the post office for twenty years."

*

The Pirates' dugout is on the first-base side of McKechnie Field, and their clubhouse is out beyond the right-field bleachers, so that's the best place to stand—along the fence—for anyone hoping to get a closer look at the players, or an autograph, or, best of all, a few words of baseball wisdom. It's now eleven forty-five, and the Pirates are taking batting practice at home plate. A few outfielders are shagging flies, a few pitchers are throwing in the bullpen, a few players are taking their turn against the pitching machine near the clubhouse. Between such tasks they can hardly help walking back and forth along the first-base line and hearing their names being called by supplicants at the railing: "Hey, Barry!" "Hey, Sid!" "Hey, Jim!" They come over and autograph whatever is held out to them and stay for a few minutes of talk—young American men talking to other American men, or to boys and girls who could be their younger brothers and sisters, or to wives and mothers and grandmothers who could be their own wives and mothers and grandmothers. Jim Leyland is hailed by various people who know him from some corner of his past, and he brightens dutifully and walks over to shake hands and maybe pose for a picture with them.

*

To have a baseball autographed it's necessary to have a baseball. At spring training the product is never far away and is often falling out of the sky.

It's now one-fifteen. The game with the Blue Jays has started and an afternoon's worth of foul balls has been set in motion. Quite a few of them land in the area behind the grandstand that includes the rest rooms and the concession stands. Many of the balls land on Ninth Street, where a small legion of boys is poised for their arrival. The boys have learned from experience the angle and trajectory at which foul pops are most likely to clear the roof of the grandstand. For some of them it's a second-generation business—their fathers did it before them. The boys sell the balls to the tourists for a dollar or two.

Across the street, in the parking lot of Superior Automotive Cleaning, I find six or seven boys waiting and watching. The lot has half a dozen shiny cars, still unclaimed by their owners, on which Superior has performed its automotive cleaning and which need nothing less than a dent inflicted by a National League ball. "There are times when you get a little aggravated, with all the balls bouncing under the cars and all the kids racing around out there," James Burke, Jr., Superior's owner, tells me. "But my attitude is 'Live and let live.' We just peacefully coexist. Kids and baseball go together."

*

Two P.M. Like the license plates on the cars parked out on Ninth Street and in the adjacent blocks, the fans are from all over America. I can read where they come from or what college or school they attend on their T-shirts or their mesh-backed caps, or I can infer it from their team loyalties; a

family of four wearing Royals baseball caps are a good bet to
be from Kansas City. I can also hear it in their conversations.
The fans are quick to make friends with people in nearby rows
and to forget all about the game for an inning or two. Nothing
is lost. The point is not to follow every play; the point is just
to *be* there—to bask again in the simple pleasures of the song
"Take Me Out to the Ball Game." Often, in fact, the game
isn't all that good. Already today I've seen several ragged throws
that pulled an infielder off his bag. They are reminders that the
perfection taken for granted by the fans is hard-won—that even
major league players need time in the winter to refine the skills
they perform with such deceptive ease in the summer.

Many of the fans are wearing Pirates caps. Some of them
come down from Pittsburgh every winter. Unlike the drop-in
tourists, they pay attention to the game, keeping score in the
program; they are looking for auguries for the new season, and
they want the Pirates to win. They also have the hometown
fan's personal interest in the players. Today the Bucs are hitting
well and the folks in the Pirates hats give them positive
reinforcement: "Way to go, Bob*beeee*!" "How to hit 'em,
Andy-baby!"

Retired couples are a big part of the crowd. They are
decorously dressed except for the colored caps with which they
proclaim a residual tie to a former employer (DEERE &
COMPANY) or a former home team up north (TWINS). They sit
in the covered grandstand, leaving the open bleachers to
younger, sun-worshiping generations. For them, spring training
is the baseball season—the only games they will actually see,
Florida having no major league clubs of its own. The rest of
the year, they will sit indoors by a TV set, watching games

being played in other states, mostly at night. Reality ends when the teams go away and start playing real games.

Between innings the fans amble down from the stands to buy hot dogs and go to the rest rooms and linger awhile to socialize; there's no better place for baseball talk than the table that holds the mustard dispenser. The men and women who work the concession stands convey the same enjoyment as the Boosters: How could anybody want to be anywhere else? Occasionally someone shouts "Heads!"—the game has resumed—and a foul ball lands among the eaters. Nobody can complain about not being close to the game as it has always been played. The fans love the ballpark ("Barb and I come here every year," "Isn't this a great little place?" "You couldn't keep us away"). Red Smith, who had a lifelong affair with McKechnie Field and wrote about it often, noted that many ex–major leaguers come back here every winter. It reminds them, he said, of a happier time when they were young and still coming up through the minors or just breaking into the big time.

*

Three-fifteen. The afternoon is so enjoyable that I keep pushing out of my mind the knowledge that what we are enjoying is a threatened and even a vanishing American pleasure. This winter alone, three clubs have moved from old spring training towns in Florida to state-of-the-art "facilities" that are bigger, colder and more corporate.

The Mets, after twenty-six years in St. Petersburg, have moved to the St. Lucie County Sports Complex, a 100-acre spread on Florida's east coast that they had built to their specifications for $13 million by a real estate corporation. "A New Town for the 21st Century," says a billboard near exit 54 on the Florida Turnpike, announcing the Mets' new spring training home, though no evidence of a town yet exists. The only conspicuous structure in a vast expanse of Florida scrub and swamp is the Mets' sleek new 7,350-seat stadium, painted Mets blue, whose field exactly matches the dimensions of their own Shea Stadium in New York, and which is encircled by practice diamonds, clubhouses, offices and other edifices so prim and urban that they could just as easily be found in Queens. The population will be along in about ten years: the developer's plans call for 15,000 homes, a luxury hotel, a huge shopping mall, an office complex, two golf courses, an elementary school and two college campuses.

The Cincinnati Reds, after fifty-four years in Tampa, not counting three years during World War II when they trained in Bloomington, Indiana, have moved to a newly built complex in Plant City, whose 6,700-seat stadium has 1,500 box seats and 3,500 reserved seats. The Kansas City Royals, after eighteen years in Fort Myers, have moved to a theme park near Orlando called Boardwalk & Baseball, where their 6,500-seat stadium ("baseball") so closely adjoins the related midway and amusement park ("boardwalk") that the shrieks and rumbles from the roller coaster and the thirty "thrill rides" often mingle with the sound of the bat. Combination tickets can be bought for the ballgame and the rides—perhaps the first time that baseball has been hawked as an "amusement" and not just as baseball. Elsewhere, the Texas Rangers have left Pompano Beach, their home since they were born in 1971, for a new complex in the "planned community" of Port Charlotte, south of Sarasota on the Gulf Coast; and the Chicago White Sox, who have long occupied a ballpark in Sarasota called Payne Park that is second only to McKechnie Field for intimacy and charm—the players have to thread a path through the fans to get from the clubhouse to the field—are building a new stadium not far away, where, it's safe to guess, such familiarity will cease.

The trend has not been overlooked by other towns and "planned communities" in Florida, suddenly aware that spring training has gone Wall Street as a growth industry. Courtiers are already out, calling on teams whose leases are almost up, and there is even talk of trying to lure to Florida some of the clubs that train in Arizona: the Chicago Cubs in Mesa, the Cleveland Indians in Tucson, the Milwaukee Brewers in Chandler, the Oakland Athletics in Phoenix, the San Diego Padres in Yuma, the San Francisco Giants in Scottsdale, and the Seattle Mariners in Tempe. Most of them are Western clubs and would therefore seem to belong at spring training camps in the West. But logic and reality have never stood in the way of people trying to sell land in Florida.

*

It's three forty-five. The game is over, and the crowd drifts out. Boys with retrieved foul balls stand at the gates and make some last-minute sales. Members of the Boosters collect the rented cushions and bring them back to the cinder-block office. The men and women in the room now remind me of people cleaning up after a church picnic.

Jack Stuhltrager introduces me to his wife, Marge, whom I

haven't seen before. "I count the money, and they let me out of the cage once in a while," she explains. I ask her where she is from.

"I grew up in a town in southern Indiana called Freetown," she says. "Don't blink when you're driving through or you'll miss it. My uncle, 'Red' Forgey, had a grocery store and a barbershop there. He also raised bird dogs, and around 1911 he happened to meet Honus Wagner, the old Pirate shortstop. Honus loved to hunt, and he started coming back every year to hunt with Uncle Red and his dogs. When Uncle Red cut people's hair he never swept the floor, so when I was a girl we just sort of assumed that Honus Wagner's hair was still there.

"We moved away, to a town called Surprise. My father had a huckster wagon and he carried all sorts of notions, like rickrack and thread. He'd go down through the hills with his wagon and sell to the hill people. After that we moved to Bicknell, which is a coal-mining region—it was mostly farm people who worked the coalfields. So I grew up in football country. We had all-state teams from that area. Our little town *was* football."

She explains that she and her first husband retired to Bradenton and were neighbors of Jack Stuhltrager and his wife. A few years ago both of them were widowed, and in 1986 she and Jack were married. Her upbringing in football country was not a helpful dowry.

"I didn't like baseball," she says, "but I liked Jack, so I thought I'd better like baseball. I went along on two Boosters trips to Pittsburgh. That's when I found out that I really loved baseball, because I could see it through Jack's eyes. And now I do once in a while know who's on third."

CHAPTER *11*

Fathers and Sons

Barry Bonds, a twenty-three-year-old outfielder with an open and likable manner, started hearing about spring training when he was hardly out of the cradle. His father, Bobby Bonds, was a star outfielder in the National League for fourteen years—notably, with the San Francisco Giants—from 1968 to 1981.

"When my dad was playing," Barry Bonds told me one day as we were standing at the edge of the field watching batting practice, "those guys made their own time. I remember hearing stories about Roberto Clemente only needing two weeks of spring training to get ready for the season. Nowadays it's different; spring training is more of an art form. It's not enough to just get in shape and take batting practice. I believe you really need that push—having the coaches around, playing other teams—to get you mentally and physically prepared. In my father's day they already *were* mentally prepared, because they were older when they were brought up to the big leagues and had been playing the game longer. Today clubs are going with the younger players, and we need the full six weeks."

Bonds, who was born on July 24, 1964, wears number 24 on his uniform, which was Willie Mays' number. Mays is his godfather and his idol. "We play golf together during the winter with my father and Willie McCovey," Bonds said. "It's nice to see those guys still active. If you put them in a game today they could still do the job—they still have the instincts and the sense of the game."

I asked Bonds whether every ballplayer needs an idol.

"I think so," he said. "In my case, between Willie Mays and George Brett and Pete Rose I find a combination of the qualities that I'd like to have myself. When I was younger I was a contact hitter, and I hit for a high average. One day my coach at Arizona State University, Jeff Pentlen, said, 'You've got all this power—how come we don't put it to use?' and he changed my swing to give me more power. So now I'm trying to combine the three great hitters that I've grown up admiring and watching constantly."

It struck me that Barry Bonds' pantheon of heroes didn't include Bobby Bonds. "Was your father also one of your idols?" I asked him.

"My father to me was my father," he said. "He was going to work. My idols were the men I was looking at playing baseball. I was looking at my dad doing his job—supporting his family. Of course, he taught me a lot, and that gave me a little bit above the other players who come into the game. I'm not saying there are many of us major league players' sons; there are only a few. What I'm saying is that we get to see both aspects of the game. You see the angry side when your father comes home after having a bad day; you see the exciting side when he comes home after he had a good day; you see him waking up in the morning and saying, 'God, I've got to go to work today.' You get to see the whole thing, and that's what gives you a head start."

Bonds picked up his bat and got ready to take his turn.

"But it's like anything else you want to do," he said. "Unless you put it to use, it doesn't work. *You* know that, being a writer—you can't go on book knowledge alone. My father could sit there day after day and say, 'This is what you can do, here's what you can expect.' But until you put that uniform on and go out there and do it you never really know what it's like."

CHAPTER 12

The Pitching Coach

Pitching is the heart of baseball—so we are always being reminded by scholars of the game, and the axiom is repeatedly proved during the endless summer, usually by negative example, as starting pitchers fail to last five innings, relief pitchers fail to hold the lead they were expensively hired to protect, and various arms succumb to orthopedic disrepair. On the whole, a team that is strong in hitting and fielding can't win a pennant if its pitching is weak. Solid pitching, on the other hand, can atone for a multitude of frailties elsewhere in the lineup. Pitchers are the margin of difference; the hopes and dreams of owners, managers, players and fans ultimately rest on that lonely figure on the mound. Perhaps no other athlete is such a delicately tuned engine of physical and mental skills or is in such demand. Anyone might think that the gene pool of the United States and its neighboring Hispanic countries would yield an adequate annual crop. It doesn't. Every year there are never enough good pitchers to go around.

This being so, one of the most important people in a spring

training camp would be the pitching coach. I didn't know much about them as a breed, though I had long watched them on TV—sage counselors standing next to the manager, studying the pitcher for signs of fatigue too subtle for the ordinary eye. Obviously they were men of saintly patience, somewhat like the trainers of highly strung racehorses, making countless trips to the box to calm the nerves of unstrung men and boys. But how did they go about their teaching?

I was in luck: the Pirates' pitching coach turned out to be Ray Miller. His was a name I knew well. During his tenure as the Baltimore Orioles' pitching coach, from 1978 to 1985, he produced two Cy Young Award winners (Mike Flanagan and Steve Stone) and five 20-game winners (Flanagan, Stone, Jim Palmer, Scott McGregor and Mike Boddecker). Baltimore twice reached the World Series in that golden age and seldom finished lower than second.

With such a record Ray Miller, I assumed, was one of baseball's venerable elders, and I scanned the field, looking for a paunch. I am haunted by the stomachs of major league coaches, for many of them are players I once saw play, and they are frozen in my memory as lithe young men. Coaches are the fan's visible link between the present and the past, and when I see them hitting fungoes or grounders before a game, hardly able to bend over to pick up the incoming ball, I can't believe that time has visited such a wry joke on them, turning them overnight into mere middle-aged American males, as overweight as any salesman or stockbroker.

But on that day in Bradenton no paunches were in sight. I would have to find Ray Miller by a more scientific method— by looking for number 31. Number 31, when I located him, was a tall, lean man in his early forties who might be taken for an associate professor of history on a college campus. He carried a clipboard and moved purposefully among the Pirate pitchers, not saying much: a word here and a word there. He had the preoccupied look of every supervisor or plant foreman—a man who had a lot to do and was serious about seeing that it got done. The more I watched him, the more I hesitated to ask for an hour of his time, and when I did he looked as if he couldn't imagine when such an hour might materialize. Finally he suggested that I meet him the next morning at eight. "I get here every day at seven-thirty," he said. "We can talk while I'm getting dressed."

The next morning I found him in the clubhouse, wearing a T-shirt that said WE WORK FAST, THROW STRIKES, CHANGE SPEEDS. He took me over to his locker, and there, putting on his uniform with slow and almost liturgical motions, he told me what I wanted to know.

*

"The first thing I look for with young pitchers in spring training," he said, "is what kind of delivery and what kind of poise they have—whether they can do something besides throw the ball hard. If they have an off-speed pitch that can deceive the hitter and if they show poise and a good delivery, I get pretty excited about them. If they have a great arm but don't have command of different pitches I kind of eliminate them from my mind, because in the big leagues a pitcher has to be able to deceive as well as to overpower. Of course, I could start to *teach* them an off-speed pitch. But my job is to get people ready who can pitch in the big leagues *now*, not people who might be able to pitch there in the future.

"The other thing is that you almost want to see a guy give up some hits and some runs. Often in spring training you have a young kid who has all the tools and he's just wiping everybody out, having a good outing every time, and you don't get a good read on what's going to happen when he gets hit. You wish he'd get into a jam to see if he can get himself out of it. Otherwise you'll never know what's going to happen when he gets in front of fifty thousand people."

Did that mean that losing is as instructive as winning? "Definitely," Miller said. "I talk to a lot of Little League groups, and I always tell them, 'Naturally all parents want their children to succeed, but a big part of life is learning to fail.' I think my job as a teacher is to keep everyone on an emotional even keel, where you're not too high with success or too dejected with defeat. Because a pitcher can do everything right, but if the fielders don't make the plays he'll frequently lose.

"So you're dealing with a highly sophisticated athletic body, and my job is to try to mentally age a young body so it can perform under pressure. I find it quite rewarding. I've been a pitching coach in the major leagues for eleven years now, and I've made an awful lot of trips from the bullpen to start a ballgame with a kid who's making his first major league appearance. No matter how hard you work for it, it's always a dream, and when you walk out onto a major league field for the first time, I don't care how much you believe in yourself, there's always that little bit of doubt: 'Well, here it goes.' "

That walk to the mound with a first-time pitcher was a ritual I had never heard of. "I never got to pitch in the big leagues myself," Miller explained, "so it's like my walk every time I do it. The biggest part of my job is to make every young kid believe that he can perform in front of a lot of people without falling apart. That's why spring training is so tough: the moment comes when you have to send them back down. We're almost at that moment now—about three weeks from opening day. We've played thirteen exhibition games and we still have nineteen pitchers here; only nine will make the team. Eight of them are set in my mind—pitchers I know I've got to get ready to pitch a season—so those eight guys are pitching more and more innings, which means there are fewer innings for the other eleven to pitch. It's hard to keep a guy up if he's not pitching and he thinks he's not going to make the team.

"When they do get cut—Jim Leyland is the one who tells them—I immediately go and talk to them. I want to keep them positive about their ability to pitch in the majors. Because in this business when you send someone down it's not like any other business in the world. When you fire a baseball player you're firing a dream—not only his dream but his family's dream and his friends' dreams, whereas in other jobs if you fire somebody they go and find another company. Here you're dealing with young egos and shattering hopes, because every kid is little Johnny from Peoria."

*

A pitching coach with a young staff can't always do things the way they ought to be done. "Last year was probably the most teaching I've ever done at the major league level," Miller said, "because the staff had so little experience. Usually those things get taught in the minors. In fact, I've always said that if you have to teach pitching at the major league level you're not going to win. And we *didn't* win. But we did come on very well near the end of the season. I was especially pleased that the guys learned to pitch on days when they didn't have really good stuff; they found they could still pitch well. So this spring we're refining all that work we did in 1987. Last year I was teaching pitches; this year I'm teaching how and when to use those pitches.

"For example, guys like Mike Dunne and Doug Drabek and Brian Fisher now have both the two-seam and the four-seam fastball. That means they've really got two pitches with one pitch. They also have a slider, a hard curve ball, a slow curve and a straight change-up. So now that they've got all those pitches, it's a question of 'When do I use them?' and 'How do I use them to set up a good hitter?' In other words, when should a pitcher change speeds? The answer is, you've got to be constantly looking for keys. Let's say you throw a good fastball and you see the batter foul it straight back. That's a key. It means that he caught up with your fastball and knows he can hit it. So now you throw with the same motion—you throw what looks like the same pitch—but it's slower, and this time he's out in front of it. It's very tough for a young kid to think about anything but himself; a lot of times he doesn't pay any attention to the hitter. And yet the hitter does all kinds of things that tell you where the bat head was when he made contact with the ball. If you have a right-handed batter and he fouls the ball over the first-base dugout, you know the bat head was way behind. So you keep throwing the ball hard. Or, obviously, if he *pulls* the ball foul you know, 'Hey, I better throw something slow—this guy's out there real quick.' "

I wondered whether there were any keys that didn't involve the bat. Miller said there were many. "Movement in the batter's box is one. A lot of guys will move up with two strikes and defend the plate, which means they're not swinging as hard. Consequently you can use your fastball more. You can see all these visual keys if you learn to look for them. We make all our starting pitchers sit next to us in the dugout during a game—except the one who's pitching—and we talk about what's going on. It's a teaching process all the time."

*

I asked Miller if it was his job to teach pitchers how to field their position. "I'm very proud of that," he said. "Usually in a spring training camp everyone keeps doing pretty much the same thing they've done for a hundred years. On covering first base, say, they practice it a few times and then they take the best players they've got and they go out and play. I don't believe in that. I think everything that happens in a game must be worked on. If you're working on something that doesn't happen in a game it's a stupid drill, because we're out here to play baseball.

"So what I do, on the fielding of bunts, for instance, is to break it down into slow motion. Most people say you just pick up the ball on the hop and throw. My method is: You bend your legs, you receive the ball, you pull it in, you look, you step, you throw." He demonstrated, making slow and deliberate movements. "By that time, of course, anybody in the world would be safe. But we're not in a game; we're practicing the fundamentals of how to field the ball. The last thing you have to do is to encourage a kid to be quick or to be strong, because he *is* quick and he *is* strong. What he's got to learn is how to do something properly at a slow speed—redundantly, a thousand times—so that when it happens at game speed he'll do it the right way by instinct. I think the Pirates field better, hold runners better and throw to bases better than any team in baseball, simply because we work on it harder."

I had noticed an arduous drill around the mound, and I asked Miller about it.

"We call that a stopped-ball drill," he said. "A baseball is just lying there in the infield, and the pitcher has to run over and pick it up and get it somewhere quickly—without going to his glove, without straightening up, without stepping. We walk through that a thousand times on the first-base side and a thousand times on the third-base side. Then the final part of the drill is this: The pitcher pitches to the catcher, and I stand behind him and drop a ball, and he's got to turn around and find it and get it to first base without going to his glove or straightening up. It sounds funny, but if you watch a baseball game those things always happen when it's important: the ball hits the pitcher, he doesn't know where it is, and he's got to locate it and go pick it up and throw the guy out. It happened yesterday in the game with the Phillies. A ball was hit back to Brian Fisher. He knocked it down and it rolled to his left. He saw it, walked over, picked it up, and threw to first just perfectly. He reacted very quickly and normally, but he did everything fundamentally right, and the reason he did—because he's been known to not be a good fielder—is that we've done it repetitively down here in spring training."

Miller said he had an extra mound and pitching rubber put in the Pirates bullpen in Three Rivers Stadium in Pittsburgh. He thought the bullpen should be more than just a warm-up place for pitchers; they should also be able to work on throwing to first base. "It's kind of dumb not to practice every day what you have to do in a game," he said. "Too many people have too many gadgets and theories and visual aids that have nothing to do with baseball. When you practice those things you're wasting your time. When you practice what happens on the field you're doing something."

*

"Do you have a set of principles that you give your pitchers at the start of spring training?" I asked Miller.

"You saw the T-shirt," he said. "Work fast, throw strikes, change speeds. That's about it. I had those shirts made up for all my pitchers. Probably the biggest complaint in baseball is that the pitcher works too slowly. In an average game—a good game—a pitcher throws 120 or 125 pitches. Some games it might be 160 pitches thrown by your team. On each one of those pitches every infielder and outfielder is taking three little steps and bracing himself for the ball to come to him. And the pitcher who works extremely slowly on a hot day in St. Louis, by the fifth inning everybody is so tired of doing it that they get mentally lazy and they don't catch a ball that's hit real close to them. But if you've got a pitcher who works fast and throws mostly strikes, everybody's anticipating more and you get better results—and not only in the field. Because more pitches are swung on, you become a better pitcher. That's no grand truth I've learned. It's just a simple fact that guys who pitch well work fast and throw strikes and change speeds. So why not teach that to young people instead of talking about all the mental factors?"

I was reminded of how often I had heard a pitcher's troubles on the mound ascribed to the fact that he was "thinking too much." (Not so Dizzy Dean: after he was famously felled by a thrown ball, the newspaper headline said, X-RAYS OF DEAN'S HEAD SHOW NOTHING.) Yet pitching is an intensely mental occupation—its practitioners have included some of the game's great eccentrics. I suggested to Ray Miller that a pitching coach must be part psychologist.

"I don't believe anyone can teach if everything he says is negative," Miller said. "Anytime you want to talk to a player about something negative, you have to first give him something positive to thrive on, and then cover the negative point in a positive context—and fast. Kids today are more worldly at eighteen than we were. They're much more affluent and they have more things to do, so when you talk to them you have to make it interesting and quick. A good history teacher makes history enjoyable, a good pitching teacher makes pitching enjoyable.

"I have a whole sequence of things that I go through all spring with my pitchers. One day I talk about one area; the next day I review it and add a little bit more, and the next day I review *that* and add a little bit more; and then we go and physically apply it, whether it's how to throw a pitch, or how to hold a runner, or whatever. It's repetitive, and yet it's simple and quick. You take them through an entire course. It's a program that you develop over the years as a pitching coach, and then during the winter you refine it. You go over your notes and consider what you think you could do more of, or less of."

One thing Miller wishes he could do better in spring training is to brief his pitchers on the hitters they will face in exhibition games. "Unfortunately, about half of those hitters aren't major leaguers," he said. "All you can do is to talk about the ones who you know *are* going to make the team. If you're playing the Mets, for instance, you tell your pitchers about the hitters they'll be seeing all summer. Of course, when the season *does* begin it's different. Every time a pitcher pitches, we keep a pitching chart in the dugout. On every pitch we mark down what kind of pitch was hit, and where it was hit, and what the count was, and other details of that kind. The next day the chart is put in the pitcher's locker, and he's supposed to write down what *he* wants to remember about the hitters he faced. Well, in our division we play each club eighteen games, so each starting pitcher might pitch three or four times against that club. In other words, I've got guys right now who have four pages of homework from last year on the Mets that they're going to face this year, and at the end of the season they'll have eight pages. What that does is to encourage every pitcher to become involved in remembering what he can successfully do against a certain hitter. I've found that if you make the pitcher do it the day after he pitches, rather than right after the game, he's more calm, regardless of what happened. Whether he was real good or real bad, when he writes his own notes they're positive. Everything I deal with is on the positive side, because it's a very negative game."

This theme of adversity had recurred so often that I wondered whether a pitcher could survive if he had an even slightly "down" personality. "Not in the major leagues," Miller said. "Too many things can go wrong that you can't control. You have to be the kind of person who can wipe it out and go right on to the next batter, optimistically. If you have any negative base in your mind you're not going to succeed, because that negative thing will happen. If you're standing on the mound with a man on second and you say, 'If I give up a base hit that guy's going to score,' he'll score. It's amazing; it just happens. But if you have a strong enough ego to say, 'The heck with that, I'll get this guy,' you'll get him. That's why you can't be a pessimist and survive.

"Usually, pessimistic people don't like what they do, and it's impossible to survive in baseball if you don't like what you do. Because you wouldn't be here if you didn't. Who wants to live on a bus for six months a year and make five hundred dollars a month and not have a job when the season's over? You can't even afford to get married, and if you do you have to drag your wife and child all around the country. Even when you do get to the major league level you're away from home for almost seven months, and even when you're home you can't do anything normal, because the schedule requires you to go on the road for two weeks and come home for two weeks, and even when you *are* home you have to be at the ballpark from two P.M. to midnight; there's no family life. So the only way to succeed is to be absolutely optimistic and love the business."

I asked Miller whether any player in his experience had made a dramatic turnaround—someone he had thought was almost out of baseball because of a down attitude.

"Just one—Steve Stone when I was with the Orioles," Miller said. "Steve was a lifetime well-under-.500 pitcher who had always played on last-place clubs, and he had developed kind of a survive-yourself-and-the-hell-with-the-team attitude. Consequently he worked real slow and he had fifty different pitches and he was always experimenting. When he joined Baltimore it was a winning club, and on a winning club you've got to let people do things their way until they ask for help. Finally Steve came to me one day and said, 'You haven't said anything much to me,' and I said, 'I think you complicate the game when you try to do everything for yourself. Would you do two things for me? One, would you work extremely fast between pitches—just get the ball and pitch, so you don't think so much? And would you reduce your five pitches to two? Choose the two best pitches you had when you warmed up, work fast, and change the speed with those two pitches.' He said, 'I'll try it.' Fortunately, he went out and won. We scored some runs for him, and he threw a shutout, and he went on to win fourteen straight games and get the Cy Young Award for the year. Steve was a little bit of a negative guy, not necessarily in his personality but because of his track record—every place he'd gone it had been lose, lose, lose. He needed one little key to get over the hump—something to make him positive. I just tried to simplify the game for him, and his ability went out and won those fourteen in a row. He had been thinking too much, and always on the negative side. What I did was to speed everything up so he didn't have so much time to think.''

*

By now Miller was fully dressed in his uniform, the didactic T-shirt no longer on display. He was also fully caught up in his subject—the joy of teaching. I asked him how he got into baseball.

"I grew up in Maryland on a tobacco farm," he said.

"Nobody in the family had ever played sports. I was probably six foot one or two when I was eleven years old, which is five inches taller than anybody else. One day I drove by a Little League field and a guy said, 'Kid, would you like to play?' and he saw me throw, and I threw real hard, and he said, 'Would you like to pitch?' and I played one game and struck everybody out, and I said, 'Boy, this is fun!' "

From that Little League debut Miller graduated to a variety of other leagues in a ten-year pitching career that took him to Salinas, Pawtucket, Dubuque, Reno, Portland, Wichita and, finally, Rochester, the Triple A farm club of the Orioles. He became the Orioles' minor league pitching instructor in 1974, was promoted to the major league club in 1979, and left in 1985 for a two-year hitch as manager of the Minnesota Twins. He joined the Pirates in the fall of 1986.

"I love to talk to successful people," he told me. "Every time I'm around a good hitter I talk to him. Or a good infielder or a good pitcher—anyone who's exceptional at what he does. I want to know what he feels and what he thinks and what he believes."

"What does that do for you?" I asked.

"They're always positive people," he said. "Most people who are extremely successful in sports keep the game at a very simple level. All the technical stuff that you hear them talk about is something they come up with because the press likes it, and the writers write it down and it sounds like a great gimmick. But most people who are good hitters or good pitchers have the innate ability to keep what's in line in line—to keep it very basic, to know, 'This is exactly what I have to do to win.' They can do all the other stuff that you want done, but basically they keep it very simple. And while they're keeping it simple they have very good keys for success, and I like to steal those keys, because I think when you're a good teacher you listen to what everybody says. In baseball there are only so many fundamental things you can do, and everybody teaches them pretty well. But another guy might present it a little bit better than you do, and if you like his way better you incorporate it in your own teaching."

The locker room was filling up with players getting dressed. "Look at those two kids," Miller said. He nodded toward two boys, one in a red shirt and one in a yellow shirt, sitting in front of their lockers staring vacantly into the middle of the room. "You can see the tension in their eyes. But there are other kids here who don't let that get to them. They have a lot of ability, and they think, 'If I'm sent down I'll be back.' I like that."

I asked Ray Miller if he had always been an upbeat person. "Always—my whole life," he said. "I refuse to ever be negative. If I'm losing ten to nothing in the ninth inning with two outs, I just know that if we get two people on we're going to win."

CHAPTER *13*

Scouts

Spring training is baseball's supreme talent show. Arrayed for six weeks on the exhibition fields of Florida and Arizona are all the players and would-be players of all twenty-six major league teams, ripe for inspection by anyone who wants to sit in the stands and watch them hit and run and field and pitch. Only the veterans know for sure that they will go north with their team when the season starts. The rest are on display, not unlike cattle at a country fair. Most of the players are on their way up—kids reaching for the main prize. Some are on their way down—men in their thirties with a residual skill, like pinch-hitting or utility infielding, that they hope will be their ticket to one more year in the majors. But what almost all of them have in common is the need to continue to catch the eye and the good opinion of a scout.

I assumed that every spring training camp was infested with scouts, if I could only find them. Surely they were solitary spies who hid in different parts of the grandstand, seeing everything and saying nothing. But when I asked about their habits I was told that they generally sit behind home plate, and one day, when the Pirates were playing the Houston Astros, I went up into the stands to look for them.

Most of the seats were occupied by fans—the usual mixture of retired couples, tourists and kids. But here and there among them I noticed men who were working—writing on long yellow pads and consulting extensive charts and tables. None of them were accompanied by women; they were sitting by themselves or with other men. They reminded me of traveling salesmen. My trail was obviously warm, and when several of the men brought out radar guns and speed guns and began to time the pitches I knew I was in scout country. What I didn't know was how to break in on their intense concentration. This was their office, and I didn't have an appointment.

Eventually a fan vacated a seat alongside a man in his mid-sixties who looked so like what I thought a scout ought to look like that I slid over next to him. If *he* wasn't a scout, nobody was. He had the blunt, weatherbeaten face of an old prizefight trainer—a face that didn't waste any energy on emotion. What caught my attention were his eyes: deep-set blue eyes that weren't missing anything on the field. He had several thick notebooks on his lap, and in his left hand he held a stopwatch that he kept clicking on and off and glancing at.

When the inning was over I introduced myself and asked him if he would tell me what he was timing. He said he was timing runners on the base paths. The answer was as laconic as the face had led me to believe it would be.

"Which base paths?" I asked.

"Mostly down to first base."

"What kind of speeds are you looking for?"

"Well, it takes a right-handed batter 4.3 seconds to reach first base," he said, "and a left-handed batter 4.1 or 4.2 seconds. Naturally that varies a little—you've got to take the human element into consideration."

"What do those numbers tell you?" I asked.

"Well, of course the average double play takes 4.3 seconds," he said. He said it as if it was common knowledge. I realized that I had never given any thought to the elapsed time of a double play. How many seconds would I have guessed? Six? Seven and a half?

"So that means . . . ?"

"If you see a runner who gets to first base in less than 4.3 seconds you're interested in him."

The break between innings was over, and the game resumed. "What other kinds of speed are you interested in?" I asked the scout.

He pointed to three men a few rows ahead of us, who were training their radar guns and speed guns toward home plate. "That last pitch was a slider," he said. "If you could read that gun from here you'd see that that pitch came in at 79 or 80 miles an hour. If the pitch had been a change-up it would have been about 73. The average fastball is 85. Those are the kinds of speeds you want to know about—how well different guys can throw different pitches."

I liked the exactitude of the numbers. As fans we swallow numbers as our daily sustenance, even if we flunked simple arithmetic at school. Our brains are clogged with statistics that define performance in exquisite gradations—earned runs and unearned runs, ordinary hits and run-scoring hits and game-winning hits—and every day we add to the data base, piecing out box scores and club standings in the morning paper like ancient runes. But now, listening to my neighbor, I realized that fans are mere communicants at the altar rail. Behind the altar there exists a whole priesthood of numbers—numbers like 4.3 and 79—that we can never hope to possess.

I asked the scout what his name was. He demurred; I sensed some scouts' code of reticence. But after we had sat together for several innings I told him I really wanted to know his name, and he gave me his card. It said that he was Nick Kamzic, Northern Scouting Coordinator of the California Angels. I asked how big the scouting staff was. He said that most major league clubs employ between fifteen and twenty full-time scouts. Assuming that almost all of them attend spring training, that meant that between four and five hundred operatives like Nick Kamzic were now sitting in ballparks in Florida and Arizona, wielding radar guns and stopwatches and pencils—a vast intelligence network going about its daily work. The thought of this network, I imagined, was never far from the minds of the marginal players, goading them to run out an infield grounder or to hustle after a foul fly—just in case somebody up there was watching.

"Essentially, we're always looking for talent," Nick Kamzic said. He explained that the main reason scouts come to spring training is not to scout the opposition but to try to find players who could plug the weak spots on their own team—players they might obtain in a trade that would benefit both clubs. A club with three shortstops, for instance, might trade one of them to a club that was shortstop-poor in return for a badly needed relief pitcher. My image of springtime scouting as a form of espionage wasn't quite right. It was more like mule trading.

Just then the ultimate mule trader, Syd Thrift, climbed up

into the stands. The crowd was thinning out, and Thrift paused to talk shop with the scouts who were there that day, his nose almost visibly sniffing for information. He knew them all. Nick Kamzic told Thrift about an Astros rookie he had been watching named Pat Keedy. "He'll hit 'em over those trees out there," he said, pointing to some palms well beyond the left-field fence. He also mentioned an Astros rookie named Cameron Drew. "During batting practice he hit that Marlboro sign," he told Thrift.

Why a California scout was telling a Pittsburgh general manager about a Houston player puzzled me; Kamzic had no equity in the situation that I could think of. But as they chatted, it occurred to me that the point of the talk was the talk itself: the pleasure that all collectors take in discussing a fine object with another addict. Kamzic and Thrift could have been two porcelain experts examining a Ming vase at Sotheby's. But I also knew that none of the information would be forgotten. Thrift would remember Keedy and Drew. Someday. . . . Thrift lumbered off, a bear looking for honey.

"You have to have a computer in your brain," Kamzic told me. "Rookies may look hot in spring training, but you never know how they're going to turn out until the bell rings. That's why I try to see them under as many different conditions as I can."

I asked him how he manages that and what kind of schedule he keeps. "I scout eleven teams on the west coast of Florida and in central Florida," he said. "I always arrive in time for the B games in the morning." B games are games that the clubs occasionally schedule so they can give some playing time to second-stringers and also get a look at rookies up from the minors for a tryout. "We already have a 'book' on most of the players in the minors," Kamzic explained. "B games give us a chance to see those minor leaguers compete against major league players, because all B games use some regulars from the major league club, especially pitchers who need to get some work in."

"Then do you also stay for the A game in the afternoon?" I asked. As soon as I asked it I knew it was a dumb question. There was no way Nick Kamzic wouldn't stick around—as long as there's a player playing somewhere, the scouting day isn't over. "Everyone's looking for catchers," he told me. "They're scarce. So are third basemen. Those are two positions I always have my eye out for."

Another inning began, and he went back to his eye work.

"He's got good motion down there," Kamzic said, nodding toward the infield, where Keedy, playing first for the Astros, had just fielded a hard grounder down the line and thrown to the pitcher for the out.

"Which one?" I asked. I thought both men had good motion. "Keedy," he said. He didn't add "of course."

I asked Kamzic whether it was his job to evaluate players who were returning from an injury or from surgery. How much could he tell about their condition? "It all depends on the anatomy of the man," he said. "They vary in their recuperative powers, and you've got to take that into account. Every player is different in how he uses his talents and his body over the course of his career. Some get better and better; others fall by the wayside. But from a scouting point of view, once a player gets established his performance is fairly constant."

As he talked, Kamzic continued to work, glancing at his

stopwatch, scribbling notes, watching the game and looking up statistics in his books of major and minor league records. I marveled that eyesight sharp enough to see a ball hitting a distant Marlboro sign could also read the tiny type in the statistical tables.

"I saw that kid in Puerto Rico," he said, pointing to another Astros rookie. "He's a nonroster player who's here for spring training, trying to make the team. His name is Jim Weaver."

"Do you also cover the Caribbean leagues?" I asked. He said he did. I hadn't expected his territory to be so broad or his year so long. I knew that scouts were a nomadic breed and that they did some of their best prospecting in remote pockets of America, on sandlot and high school and college diamonds. Baseball lore abounds with stories of scouts sitting in an Iowa kitchen or an Oklahoma barn talking to the parents of kids with names like Bob Feller and Mickey Mantle. But I thought the work was seasonal and fairly local.

"When do you get a vacation?"

"I get the holidays off," Kamzic said. "It's an all-year-long job, just like everybody else's job."

*

I asked Kamzic how long he had been a scout and how he got into the business.

"This is my fortieth year," he said. "Originally I was a shortstop. In 1941 I went from the D League to the Triple A in one summer. The Triple A team was Green Bay, and at the end of the season I was signed by the Milwaukee Brewers. But in 1942 I was drafted into the army. I was with the Ninety-fifth Division of Patton's Third Army, and I was wounded in combat twice. When the war was over I tried to come back, and I went through a long period of rehabilitation. But after four years your timing is off. Finally I had to face the fact that I just wasn't going to make it back from those war injuries, and in 1948 I became a scout—first with the Reds for ten years, then with Milwaukee, and finally with the Angels. I've been with the Angels for twenty-seven years."

"What does it take to be a scout?"

"Judgment," Kamzic said. "Every scout keeps his own book, and every scout has a different opinion. But what the club wants is *your* opinion and nobody else's. That's what they're paying me for. You can't beat experience."

The game had reached the ninth inning. Both Jim Leyland and Hal Lanier had made a large number of substitutions, sending rookies into the lineup as pinch-hitters and infielders and outfielders, using the game for its classic spring training purpose. Nick Kamzic's pad was half filled with writing; by the end of spring training he would have amassed as many field notes as an anthropologist returning from a study. He was a walking encyclopedia. I wondered what he did with all his research.

"I make regular reports to the Angels' front office," he said, "and then I take all my records home." Home is Evergreen Park, Illinois—a location he chose for two reasons. "First," he said, "it's in the heart of America. Also, it's not far from Chicago. Chicago is a two-team city, so all the clubs from both leagues have to come through there. By making my home in Evergreen Park I can keep track of every team."

Out on the field, a Pirate fielder caught an Astros fly to end the game. Nick Kamzic put away his stopwatch and bundled up his archives. Around us, the other scouts packed their speed guns. None of them had left before the last out.

"I think scouts are the key people in baseball," Kamzic said as we left the grandstand. "They're the ones who get the players. Scouts and ballplayers are like ham and eggs. There wouldn't be any scouts without ballplayers and there wouldn't be any ballplayers without scouts."

CHAPTER *14*

A Ton of Ground Balls

Watching a well-executed double play is one of the pleasures of an American summer, as refreshing as a lemonade or a dip in the ocean, and I got an early start on this indulgence at McKechnie Field as I watched the Pirate infielders polishing their art in daily drills, refining the pivot and throw at second base, and incessantly scooping up ground balls. The drillmaster was Tommy Sandt, the Bucs' first-base coach, who is in charge of the infielders.

At thirty-seven, Sandt is the youngest of the club's young coaches, sharing with Gene Lamont a background of playing only briefly in the major leagues—42 games at shortstop for the Oakland A's—but serving a long tenure in the minors as a player and manager. Most recently he managed the Hawaii Islanders, Pittsburgh's Triple A club in the Pacific Coast League, twice winning the divisional championship, and he was promoted to the Pirates in 1986. With his bushy, straw-colored mustache, he resembles the ballplayers of an earlier era, and his ruddy face has been burnished by twenty years of sun in

Burlington, Birmingham, Tucson, New Orleans, Syracuse, Portland, Lynn, Buffalo and Honolulu. It was a face that reminded me that baseball is still an outdoor occupation and that it still imposes hard migratory labor on men who played briefly in the majors but dream of making it back as coaches or managers—of rediscovering the miracle of big crowds, first-class hotels, good food and decent transportation.

Jim Leyland, the product of just such an odyssey himself, had been in his late thirties when he was third-base coach of the Chicago White Sox, and when he became manager of the Pirates he chose men of roughly that age for his own coaches. "Coaching is a facet of the game that interests me," Leyland explained. "In this business it's easy to find someone with many years of experience who knows a great deal but who physically can't do a lot of work anymore, and it's also easy to find a young guy who's gung ho but who doesn't yet have the knowledge or the experience to be effective. What's very tough is to find a guy who knows a lot and who can also work hard. That's what we've got here. All our coaches are in the same age bracket, they're all knowledgeable, and they've all played in the big leagues or have managed for a long time in the minor leagues and have a great deal of experience. So I'm really lucky, because the way this club is constructed we've got so many young players that I need my coaches to get down there in the pits with them."

Sandt was very much a pit-dweller. "As a teacher I really believe in working one on one," he told me. "I love to be with one or maybe two guys and to be able to demonstrate what I mean. If I can do it myself I'll take a ground ball or turn a double play—whatever I'm trying to teach at that time. But if something comes up that I physically can't do I'll get someone who *can* do it—someone who I know can show the person how to execute it right. You can tell somebody to do something all day long, but until they've *seen* it it's not going to help them much."

Like his fellow coaches, Sandt seemed to be working to some inner clock—one whose alarm would go off on opening day. "To me the big thing about spring training," he said, "is that everybody needs to refresh himself, no matter who he is or how long he's been around, whether he's a manager or a player or a coach. In October you go home and sit for five months, and when you start spring training you think, 'Now, how did we *do* that?' It'll come back to you, but it's not a natural thing. There are a lot of points you've just got to think about. That's why you work on it. There's no other way.

"Basically, down here we work on good fielding fundamentals. When you've got an artificial surface, as we do at home in Pittsburgh, you can get lazy and do some things wrong and still catch the ball—you get two nice hops every time, there are no tricky bounces, and the ball is always up pretty high to you. But down here on grass and dirt you get five or six hops, so you've got to get your fundamentals right. You've got to get down on the ball, and watch it into the glove, and get your hands out in front of your body, and be in balance. So it's good that we've got real grass down here in spring training."

Watching Sandt as he plied his infielders with grounders, I wondered how much practice they could profitably take. "The biggest thing," he said, "is that you can't do it too long. You don't need to get someone out there to take ground balls for an hour. It doesn't do any good. First of all, they get bored

and they don't concentrate. They also get tired, and when you
get tired that's when you create bad habits, whether you're
taking fielding practice or batting practice or whatever you're
doing. Sometimes you have to get tired to go a *little* bit farther.
But when you get real worn out you get lazy and start doing
things badly. So I keep it to about fifteen or twenty minutes.
And I'll do the same thing after the season begins. I'll tell them,
'You don't have to take three thousand ground balls today;
just go out and work on your double play, work on your
backhand, work to your left'—whatever I think they need.
You've got to keep it fresh for them and come up with new
ideas, so it's not just a chore every day. There's an old saying,
'You play like you practice.' If you do it so that it becomes a
daily grind you pick up bad habits, and that's the way you're
going to play."

I told Sandt about my fondness for the sight of a shortstop
and a second baseman making a double play. I said I assumed
that such finesse could only be achieved by long practice.

"I had two guys when I was managing the Pirates' club in
Lynn," Sandt said, "who got so good that they practiced
turning double plays without looking. They would close their
eyes and do it. On a ground ball to the shortstop, the first guy
would catch it and then close his eyes and throw to second,
and when the second baseman caught the ball he'd close his
eyes and throw to first. After you've practiced enough you
don't even need to look at first base—you just wing the ball
and it gets over there. But it's all practice; it's a rhythm that
you get."

"Who were those guys?" I asked.

"The shortstop was Rafael Belliard, who's with us on the

Pirates now, and the second baseman was Nelson Norman, who's with our Buffalo Triple A club. Then they would switch positions and do the same thing. They were amazing."

*

One of the classic uses of spring training is to convert a player to a new position, and Sandt had a classic conversion on his hands: to make a third baseman of Bobby Bonilla. Few spring training tasks were more important to the club's future. Early in the 1987 season Bonilla was thought to be a hitter of great potential, but he had no regular position; he was a part-time first baseman and right fielder. Midway through the season a decision was made to install him at third base—Syd Thrift hadn't forgotten that he tried Bonilla there during the high school all-stars' Scandinavian tour—and Bonilla played the Pirates' last 75 games at third. "One reason we wanted to move Bobby last summer," Sandt said, "was that we thought he'd hit better if we could settle him in one place, and that's exactly what happened." After the All-Star break Bonilla hit .307 and led the club in runs batted in, wrapping up the year of his conversion with a .357 average in his last 46 games.

On-the-job training, however, is not the ideal way to learn a new position, especially one that requires so many kinds of quickness, and in 1988, when the Pirates arrived in Bradenton for spring training, Sandt went at the job more pedagogically. I had noticed him hitting an infinite variety of grounders to Bonilla at third base when everybody else's working day was over. "You don't mind if Bobby gets a little fatigued doing it

during spring training," Sandt said. "You just don't want to
tire him out with that kind of drill during the season." Bonilla
didn't look like a man who would tire easily—he is six feet
three and weighs 230 pounds. He also didn't look compact
enough to be a third baseman.

That didn't bother Sandt. "Bobby's got quick hands and a
strong arm," he said, "and he's pretty agile for a big guy. You
need soft hands to play third base. Guys who don't have soft
hands jab for the ball, and that leads to a lot of errors. The
biggest thing is to get your footwork right; if you have slow
feet, your hands are no good. What I mainly want Bobby to
learn is how to read a ground ball. It's important to get the
hop you want, not to let the ball make you play *its* hop. One
thing I've been doing, instead of hitting ground balls to him
with a fungo, is to use a regular bat and get somebody to lob
pitches to me. That's more realistic if you're learning the
position. Third base is tough—it's all reaction. I'm also working
with Bobby on different ways to go to first base. Guys who
are new at third need to know that you don't have to gun the
ball over every time. Most of all, it's a matter of getting
comfortable with where you're going to be playing every day.
It affects a player's entire game."

Bonilla was one of the players the fans at McKechnie Field
most wanted to see. His impressive finish in 1987 had stamped
"future star" all over him. Now, at twenty-five, a man with a
strong and graceful body and an open face that smiled easily,
he appeared to be totally loose and to have no tension
whatever. "I just want to have some fun," he said when I asked
him if Sandt's drills were difficult, and he was serious about it.
I felt that he was a player who would never kill his natural gifts

with undue worry or self-reproach—there would always be another game.

"The hardest part of moving to third base was not the transition itself," Bonilla said. "The tough part was quickening my footwork. At first base you can usually kneel down and keep a ground ball in front of you and flip it to the pitcher. At third you don't have that luxury; you've got to throw it. So Syd Thrift brought an instructor down here named Frank Raines, who has worked with the Washington Redskins. He made me see that the first step you take is the most important one, and once he had quickened my footwork I was more at ease. I've also been doing a lot of extra work with Tommy Sandt. You've got to put in the hours. Every day Tommy hits me a ton of ground balls. He hits them to me until I'm wobbling. Till I'm *wobbling!* Then he says, 'Are you ready to start now?'

"But at a certain point you have to get in some game situations to really put yourself at ease. It's more of a confidence factor than being able to catch a ground ball. The most important thing about my transition to third base is that I *wanted* to play third base. When you want to do something you're more relaxed at it and you learn more. I saw it as an opportunity to play every day and have some fun."

"What does spring training mean to you?" I asked him.

"Spring training," he said, "reacquaints you with the things you tend to forget once the season is over." He repeated the word slowly, breaking it into three syllables for emphasis: "It re-ac-*quaints* you." It was as good a word to define spring training as I would get. "That's why it's so repetitious," he said.

Probably nobody in the Pirates' camp was having a more

repetitious time of it than Bonilla, fielding ground balls until he wobbled. But nobody looked more free of care. In his spare moments I had seen him fulfilling the duties of a rising star—signing autographs and talking to clusters of reporters and fans—and I asked him whether he liked this aspect of his new celebrity or found it a burden.

"I like everything about the game," he said.

CHAPTER 15

Calling on Edd Roush

One of the first things I wanted to do when I got to Bradenton was to try to call on Edd Roush, who, at ninety-four, was the oldest living member of the Baseball Hall of Fame. Roush had been a winter resident of Bradenton for thirty-six years and was thus its patron saint of baseball, a familiar presence during spring training at McKechnie Field, where he held court on a special couch out in left field and told everyone how much better the game was played in his day.

I could hardly believe the good luck that had delivered to my chosen city one of baseball's authentic giants. As an outfielder with the Cincinnati Reds and the New York Giants for sixteen seasons, from 1916 to 1931, Edd Roush hit over .300 twelve times, hit over .350 in three successive seasons, twice won the National League batting championship, and compiled a lifetime average of .323. Defensively he was no less exceptional—historians of the game rank him with Tris Speaker, Joe DiMaggio and Willie Mays. "That Hoosier moves with the regal indifference of an alley cat," said his last manager,

John McGraw, who once suffered the indignity of signaling to
Roush to shift position in center field, whereupon the batter
lined a triple through the vacated spot. When the inning was
over, McGraw said to Roush, "Next time I signal you to move,
don't budge."

I knew that Roush had been notoriously cantankerous in his
playing days—he was probably the only player who talked back
to McGraw and got away with it—and I gathered from
reporters on the *Bradenton Herald* that he was no less testy at
ninety-four, especially with people he felt were pestering him.
That didn't augur well for my getting an interview. Still, I was
determined to try—no older link to the National League's past
glory would come my way. I also had a strong sense of time
running out.

Not wanting to risk being rejected on the phone, I found
out where Roush lived and drove around to his house. It was
a modest white one-story house in a modest residential section
of Bradenton. The small lot had two orange trees and a neatly
lettered mailbox that said EDD J. ROUSH. But there was no car
in the carport and no sign of life. The woman next door was
raking her yard, and I asked her if she knew where Mr. Roush
had gone and when he would be back.

"He'll be away for two weeks," she said. "He went to the
funeral of his twin brother."

The sentence stunned me. It wasn't just the idea of two
Indiana farm boys living to almost ninety-five. I also had a
hunch that twins were genetically programmed in the same
way. Now time was really running out. I made a note of the
date when Roush was expected back and began my vigil. My
thoughts kept returning to the white house with the mailbox.

Every morning, the first thing I did was to open the newspaper to the obituary page. No news continued to be good news, and when the two weeks were up I drove out to the house again. I chose ten o'clock for my second strike.

This time there was a car in the carport. The house had no doorbell—a deterrent to pesterers, I assumed—so I knocked on the kitchen door. After several minutes it was opened by a stern-looking woman in her seventies, who said she was Edd Roush's daughter, Mary Allen. I explained my mission. She said she had heard about it. "Some damn fool from the newspaper called," she said, "to tell me that a big writer from New York was in town to do a story about Edd Roush." She stayed on her side of the screen door.

"We don't like to have writers sicced on us," Mrs. Allen said. "There are three things my dad has no use for—preachers, teachers and writers. That's why it took him until 1962 to get into the Hall of Fame—the baseball writers weren't about to vote for him. He had to wait until the old-timers committee voted him in. Of course, he couldn't care less if he got in the Hall of Fame." She started to close the kitchen door.

Talking fast, I told Mrs. Allen that I hadn't been sicced on her and her father by anyone—that I was acting on my own as a writer. "I'm mainly here to pay my respects to Mr. Roush," I said. I explained that my book wasn't about Edd Roush; it was about spring training and Bradenton, and I didn't think it would be right for such a book not to have anything in it about her father.

Mary Allen looked at me long and hard through the screen door. Finally she turned around and I heard her say, "You might as well let him in, Dad. He's here anyway." She unlocked the door and pushed it open. "You can have ten minutes," she said.

Until that moment I had been so intent on getting into the house that I hadn't given much thought to what its famous occupant would look like. I think I expected to find a frail old man wearing slippers, quite possibly still in his pajamas. I thanked Mrs. Allen and went in.

The living room was small and very neat, and in the middle of the room a small and very neat man was sitting straight up in a chair. The oldest living member of the Baseball Hall of Fame was wearing a freshly cleaned and pressed khaki shirt, freshly cleaned and pressed khaki trousers, socks, and shined shoes. His hair was wet-brushed down, and he looked at me with vigilant blue eyes. Another damn-fool writer, they said. I shook hands as ceremoniously as if I were meeting royalty—which I was. The hands and wrists were still large—farmer's hands and wrists, unreduced by age. These were the hands, I remembered, that had swung the heaviest bat ever used in major league baseball—forty-eight ounces.

I pulled up a chair and set my mental timer at ten minutes. More probably, I thought, it would be eight or nine—Mary Allen was hovering at the edge of the room. I asked Edd Roush to tell me about his ties to Bradenton. He said he had first come down in 1952, by trailer. "If you didn't like your neighbors you could move," he explained. Subsequently he built the house we were in now, and he and his daughter had spent their winters there ever since. They spent the other six months in Oakland City, Indiana, the small town where Roush grew up—and, incidentally, first played ball, in 1910, for the Oakland City Walk-Overs. The family farm had long since been sold, and Roush and Mrs. Allen now lived on Main Street.

I asked Roush what he remembered about spring training in his playing days. "Spring training!" he scoffed. "I was a holdout every year so I wouldn't have to do it. I never came down until a week before the team broke camp. I only needed a couple of swings and I could hit with any of 'em. I was always in shape— I was born and raised on a farm; my dad ran a dairy in Oakland City."

Another reason for avoiding spring training, he said, was that the ballparks were little better than cow fields, full of holes. Why go to spring training to break an ankle? I asked him if he could remember any of those early Florida parks. "There was one in Miami," he said, "about a mile out of town. We players stayed at a hotel in the city and got out to the park by jitney. The jitney was a Model-T Ford, and the fare was five cents." But even in the major leagues, he said, "they didn't fix ballparks up the way they do now. The one in Brooklyn had rocks in the outfield. Every time I came back to the dugout I had a handful of pebbles." He was talking about Ebbets Field.

I asked Roush if he enjoyed watching today's spring training games at McKechnie Field. The blue eyes flared with anger. "Don't ask me about these modern players," he said. "If they had come out to the park when *I* was playing, we'd have run 'em out of town. These fellers bat .265 and think they're hitters. Their gloves are as big as two of ours and they still can't catch the ball. And they're millionaires!"

The thought of today's big salaries riled him, and he was reminded of his own famous effort to extract more money from John McGraw's Giants in 1927, after that club got him from Cincinnati. Roush had worked for McGraw once before—as a rookie in 1916—and both men had never forgotten it. McGraw couldn't forget that he had traded Roush to the Reds early in the season and watched him tyrannize the league with his forty-eight-ounce bat for the next eleven years; ever since, he had wanted him back. Roush couldn't forget how abusive McGraw had been as a manager and had sworn never to play for him again. Therefore, when he received a Giants contract for $19,000, the same salary the Reds had paid him, he mailed it back. Two subsequent contracts, for $20,000 and $21,000, were greeted with equal scorn. Roush let it be known that nothing less than $30,000 could induce him at this late hour to put up with the verbal lashings of John J. McGraw; he would rather be quail-hunting, and that's what he did while the Giants went south for spring training.

Just before the season started, a peace conference was arranged in a hotel room in Chattanooga. Roush recalled the meeting for me as if the sixty-one years had never passed:

"McGraw said, 'I'm not near as bad as I used to be. You play your game out there and I'll never say a word to you.' I told him, 'All managers say that; then when the player is signed they do what they've always done.' I told him I wasn't going to come down from $30,000. And there was hardly a darn soul who was getting over $14,000 at that time; I think the only one was Rogers Hornsby. McGraw said he couldn't pay me that much. I got up and started to leave. He said, 'Wait a minute—here's what I'll do. I'll give you $75,000 for three years.'

"I said, 'I'm not going to be with you very long anyway, so I might as well sign it. But the first time you give me any trouble I'm going home to Indiana.' Well, I played for that man for three years and he didn't say a word to me. And I always had to sit next to him on the bench—that was the only seat left when I got back in from the outfield."

Actually McGraw broke his vow of silence several times—
most notably, judging by how vividly Roush recalled it, on the
occasion of Cincinnati's first trip to New York in 1927. "I was
out on the field during batting practice, talking to some of my
old friends on the Reds," Roush told me. "The clubhouse at
the Polo Grounds was out in center field, and McGraw must
have been sitting out there by the window, watching everything. When practice was over, McGraw come to me and he
says, 'Roush, I saw you socializing with the opposition.
Nobody does that on my team.'

"I told him, 'I played with those fellers for eleven years. I'm
not going to ignore them.' "

Mary Allen announced that my ten minutes were up. But
Edd Roush had a point that he wanted to make. "When I
played that game," he said, "I played to win." He looked at
me with his intense blue eyes. "I told McGraw, 'When this
ball game starts, all friendship ceases.' "

*

Mary Allen didn't kick me out immediately,
so I followed her into the kitchen and asked her about her own
life. She said she had been a schoolteacher in small towns in
and around Oakland City. I mentioned that I had also done
some teaching in southern Indiana, at colleges and writers'
conferences, and soon it was as if there had never been a screen
door between us. I asked her whether it was a burden to be a
Hall of Fame ballplayer or a member of the family.

"Just last year some fool put Dad's address in one of those
collectors' magazines," she said, "and we started being really
hounded for autographs. So my grandson, Jade Roush

Dellinger—he's over at the University of South Florida—said he thought his great-grandfather ought to start charging money for his autograph. He said he thought Bob Feller had been doing it for years and probably most of the other Hall of Famers too. Jade figured it would put an end to people bothering us. So we had this notice typed up and mimeographed." She gave me a small piece of white paper that said:

EDD J. ROUSH IS NOW THE OLDEST LIVING MEMBER OF THE BASEBALL HALL OF FAME. DUE TO HIS AGE, AND THE COMMERCIALIZATION OF BASEBALL MEMORABILIA, MR. ROUSH NOW CHARGES FOR SIGNATURES:

HALL OF FAME PLAQUES AND REGULAR CARDS	$5.00 EA
PEREZ-STEELE CARDS	$7.50 EA
BASEBALLS	$15.00 EA
PHOTOGRAPHS	$10.00 EA

MR. ROUSH DOES NOT SIGN BATS.
THANK YOU FOR YOUR COOPERATION.

Far from holding back the flood, the newly announced rates quickened the collectors' appetites, and they began sending such a profusion of items to be autographed that Mrs. Allen started to keep an account so that she wouldn't get in trouble with the Internal Revenue Service. She brought a big ledger over to the kitchen table. Many pages were already filled with names, addresses and amounts.

"Look at this," she said. "From the time we got down here in Bradenton on October 13, through December 31, the total is $2,976.50. You wouldn't believe some of the stuff people

send. Last week the mailman brought a big box, and we got it
unpacked and it was the slat of a seat from some stadium in
New Jersey that got torn down. The man said he was sending
them to all Hall of Famers. Well, there's no way Dad was
going to sign *that*. If he signed that, they'd send him a pair of
shoes that they'd claim he wore; they'd be saying 'These are
his authentic shoes' next. We packed the thing up and sent it
right back."

I heard the screen door open and saw Edd Roush go out
into the backyard. I told Mrs. Allen I thought he looked pretty
spry. "He's had one stroke and any number of heart attacks,"
she said. "There was one last summer out in Oakland City that
had me real upset. But Dr. Brink of Princeton, Indiana, said,
'Don't worry about him, Mary—he's too ornery to die.' He
has at least six beers every day. Last month at the Governor's
Dinner in St. Petersburg, which was held to celebrate the
hundredth year of spring training in Florida, he sat up on the
dais like George Burns, smoking cigars. He's always been
independent-minded. He had sense enough to put his money
in stocks, not to build a big house, and always to buy Ford
cars."

I asked Mrs. Allen if I could look at her ledger to see where
the requests for autographs were from.

"Here's one I just couldn't figure out when it came in," she
said, pointing to a late November entry. "We got thirty-six
baseballs from Lebanon, Indiana. At fifteen dollars per
autograph, that's five hundred and forty dollars. The check was
from a man named William Daniels in Zionsville. Now, there's
no way that man could sell thirty-six baseballs in Lebanon; they
don't even have a jail—it's that little a town. I wouldn't know

that if I hadn't taught school in Elmwood, which is real close. Finally I remembered that there are a lot of small home-owned tool-and-die factories in that area, and I guessed that Mr. Daniels owned one of them. Probably he wanted to give those baseballs to his employees as Christmas presents."

I heard the screen door open again. Edd Roush was going back to his chair.

"Would you like to see what goes out of here in a typical day's mail?" Mrs. Allen asked. I said I certainly would. "Come on," she said. "I don't think the mailman has come yet."

We walked out to the mailbox, which Mrs. Allen had stuffed earlier that morning with outgoing items. Most of them were lumpy self-addressed packages that the collectors had enclosed for the return of their autographed baseballs. Mrs. Allen pulled them out of the mailbox and handed them to me. I sat down on the grass to read the day's destinations: East Petersburg, PA; Roanoke Rapids, NC; West Deal, NJ; Little Rock, AR; Center, MO; Canterbury, CT; Mahwah, NJ; Centralia, MO; Virginia Beach, VA; Bristol, TN; and Brooklyn, NY.

I wadded everything back in the mailbox and started to say goodbye to Mary Allen. My ten minutes had stretched into an hour. Just then the mailman's jeep arrived. The mailman pulled all the oddly shaped packages out of the box, put a new load of oddly shaped packages in, waved to Mary Allen and drove off. She and I reached in to see what the day's tide had washed up: twelve packages and envelopes, from Idaho, Maine and various states in between. The biggest envelope, elaborately stamped DO NOT BEND, was from Forty Fort, PA.

I helped Mary Allen carry the mail in to the kitchen. Then I went back to the living room and said goodbye to Edd Roush.

He was sitting straight up in his chair, staring fiercely into the past.

Six days later Edd Roush died. He had a heart attack at McKechnie Field, just before a game between the Pirates and the Royals.

CHAPTER 16

Three Pitchers

Jeff Robinson looks more Ivy League than National League. Blond and blue-eyed, he could be a newly fledged M.B.A. Instead, at twenty-seven, he is one of the most vexing relief pitchers in the game, giving the Pirates, along with Jim Gott, two almost unstoppable stoppers. He came to Pittsburgh late in the 1987 season from the San Francisco Giants, bringing with him a full arsenal of pitches, the most lethal being the split-fingered fastball, which he learned from the Giants manager, Roger Craig. Craig has taught that sharply dipping pitch to so many pitchers who have since gone elsewhere that it is now a menace from coast to coast. Robinson would have been an apt pupil at Craig's split-finger academy; describing the timetable of spring training, he was as analytical as a management consultant.

"In the off season," he said, "I'll get my*self* in physical condition in order to come to spring training. Then in spring training I'll get my *arm* in condition. I'll start out by just getting its strength back. Then, because I'm a relief pitcher, I have to get

The modest main gate at McKechnie Field is matched by the modest admission prices at the ticket window. The ballpark opens at eleven—not a moment too soon for fans who want to watch batting practice and talk to the players. (Carson Baldwin)

The railing along the first-base line is the ideal spot for Pirate-watching. Players and coaches going back and forth between the diamond and the clubhouse in right field are easy prey for autograph-stalkers. The scoreboard in center field provides the line score and doesn't do anything else. (Carson Baldwin)

Game time is still an hour away, but there's no shortage of codgers and tourists in the stands, none of them in any hurry. Many are from the Midwest, and they are quick to strike up friendships with other "snowbirds" from "up North." The lofty perch at the right is the press box. (Carson Baldwin)

The covered grandstand behind home plate is a favored roost of retired couples who actually want to stay out of the sun and for scouts from other clubs, who sit in the front rows with radar guns, timing the pitchers' pitches and judging whether they've got it, have lost it, or will never have it. (Carson Baldwin)

General manager Syd Thrift. Summing up the purpose of spring training, he notes, "In the Book of Hosea it says, 'My children shall perish for lack of knowledge,' and I believe totally in that philosophy."

Pirate manager Jim Leyland. The tone of spring training, he says, "is always just a good old-fashioned hard day's work."
(Carson Baldwin)

Syd Thrift, in characteristic spring training garb, expounds one of his theories to manager Jim Leyland. Thrift says,"I told them all up front: 'I'm a hands-on general manager.'"

Coach Ray Miller.

Coach Gene Lamont.

Coach Tommy Sandt.

Coach Milt May.
(Carson Baldwin)

Tommy Herr of the St. Louis Cardinals signing autographs before a game with the Pirates. The supplicants at the rail represent most of the seven ages of man—a typical sample of who comes to spring training. Eleven different clubs from both major leagues played exhibition games at McKechnie Field during the Pirates' Grapefruit League season. (Carson Baldwin)

Jack Stuhltrager, president of the Bradenton Pirates Boosters, wearing the cap that identifies this genial clan, selling the official program to arriving fans. With proceeds from their programs and rented seat cushions, the Boosters have put $110,000 worth of improvements into McKechnie Field. (Carson Baldwin)

Trainer Kent Biggerstaff with the Cybex machine that examines every Pirate player when he arrives for spring training. It tests all the major joints, makes a printout of muscle strength, and identifies specific weaknesses. Twenty years ago, Biggerstaff says, "mostly what you'd find in the training room was horse liniments." (Carson Baldwin)

Umpire Frank Pulli. In spring training, he says, "you want to show yourself, and then you want to show the players, that you haven't lost it. You're pumped up." (Louis Requena)

The great outfielder Edd Roush, oldest member of the Baseball Hall of Fame and a longtime winter resident of Bradenton, was a familiar presence at McKechnie Field. This picture of Roush in his glory days with the Cincinnati Reds was probably taken around 1920. He says he told John McGraw, "When this ball game starts, all friendship ceases." (The New York Times)

Scout Nick Kamzic, one of the several hundred scouts from all twenty-six major league clubs who make their rounds of the spring training camps. "There wouldn't be any scouts without ballplayers," Kamzic says, "and there wouldn't be any ballplayers without scouts."

Relief pitcher Jeff Robinson in the Pirate bullpen in right field with one of his young fans, probably demonstrating the grip on his killer pitch, the split-fingered fastball. (Carson Baldwin)

*Center fielder
Andy Van Slyke.*

*Third baseman
Bobby Bonilla.*

*Relief pitcher
Jim Gott.*

*Catcher
Mike LaValliere.*

*Left fielder
Barry Bonds.*

Pitcher Doug Drabek.

First baseman Sid Bream.

Pitcher Mike Dunne.

Pitcher Bob Walk.

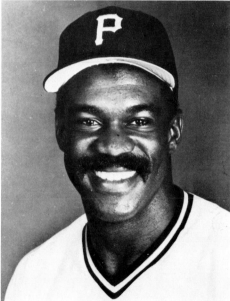

Right fielder
R. J. Reynolds.

my arm conditioned to pitch every single day. My individual pitches come back to me in successive stages. For instance, I throw a sinking fastball, and it takes a couple of weeks for my fingers to get strong enough to throw it. Then it's another three or four days until I get my slider down, and after that it's another couple of days until I get my split-fingered fastball down. That's where I am now. We've got two weeks to go and I'm almost at one hundred percent. I can control all my pitches and I have the strength and resilience that I'll need during the season."

Another kind of strength and resilience that Robinson would need would be psychological. What kind of training does it take to prepare for baseball's equivalent of working in a hospital emergency room? The stopper gets called only to stop the bleeding, bind up the wounds and apply a tourniquet.

"It's hard to prepare for the psychological pressure of being a relief pitcher," Robinson said, "because during spring training you're never really in a pressure situation. I'm not down here to try to prove to anybody what I'm all about. I'm here to get in shape, and do my proving during the season. When you're trying to make the team it's different; the manager and the coaches are going to put you out there in a pressure situation so they can find out how you'll act, because there's a big difference between having five thousand people in the stands down here in Florida and forty thousand people in the stands up North.

"Another kind of pressure you can't prepare for down here is all the media attention you get after the season begins. You have a lot more questions to answer if you do well in a game—

and also if you do badly. You can only try to be fair to those reporters and hope they'll be fair to you.''

*

Brian Fisher, a right-handed relief pitcher of sporadic success for the Yankees in 1985 and 1986, was converted into a starter by the renascent Pirates of 1987 and became a solid member of the staff, along with Doug Drabek, who was acquired from the Yankees in the same trade. A tall and well-built young man, just twenty-six, Fisher told me he was using spring training to try to cure a problem that wouldn't be easy to fix once the season began.

"I have a problem with closing myself off on the mound," he said. "I step, and my body's a little closed. What I mean by that is that my front toe is turned more toward third base than toward home plate, and it's been getting worse and worse. I have a bad left knee anyway—I have some chips and a couple of spurs right on top of my patella. I'm also a little bit pigeon-toed. So we've been changing my foot around. We've been working on getting my front foot—my landing foot—to point forward, and it helps out quite a bit. I can open up and throw the ball harder now and also throw my slider better. I can also see the ball better when it's hit back to me. In the past I haven't been in a good position to field my position, and consequently I've missed a lot of hits that I should have gotten. But in yesterday's game I fielded four balls that were hit right back to me."

I asked Fisher how he had diagnosed his problem.

"Ray Miller pointed it out last year in the middle of the season," he said, "and we started working on it. But you're reluctant to tinker with that sort of thing during the regular schedule. Down here, if you make some mistakes in a game it doesn't count for a whole lot. For instance, what I've been doing in my games this spring is to check my landing spot after each pitch—checking to make sure my toe was still open, and if it wasn't, to remind myself of it before the next pitch. During the season you're concentrating so hard on getting the job done that you don't think about those things."

How often had I heard the cliché about baseball being a game of inches? No more than a few thousand times. These were inches, however, that I had never heard about—the slight variations in a pitcher's foot direction.

"What you try to do in spring training," Fisher said, "is get to where everything becomes natural, so that when the season begins you're not worrying about your motion or your mechanics. You're just trying to throw your pitches where you want them. In many ways spring training is the best part of the year, because you get a chance to correct your mistakes and go on from there. You're not in a do-or-die situation."

*

Jim Gott is only twenty-eight, but he seems older than his teammates, perhaps because he has been in the major leagues longer than any of them—six years—but more probably because he is one of those young men who seem to have been born mature. There is nothing of the fraternity jock about him; Gott is every class president—outgoing, enormously sincere, eager to be helpful and involved. I felt this so strongly when I met him that I wasn't surprised to learn later that he was already active in many Pittsburgh charities, though he had only been with the club for six months.

Gott has good reason to believe in the powers of faith and reclamation: he was almost a charity case himself. Given up on by the Giants and every other club, he was acquired by the Pirates in August 1987 for the bargain-basement price of fifty thousand dollars. His career appeared to be over. Thereupon he became the club's ace stopper—the heart of the bullpen, along with Jeff Robinson, that was widely credited for the Pirates' winning 27 of their last 38 games in 1987. When I caught up with Gott in spring training he had just come back from a brief leave to be with his wife while she was having a baby, and he was in a thoughtful mood.

"We're playing the Blue Jays today, and my first major league spring training was with them, back in '82," he said, "so I was just reflecting back on that a few minutes ago, talking to some of my former friends over there. I remember so clearly how hard it was as a young pitcher to stop thinking about all the mechanical moves that the coaches had been talking to you about. That's the last thing you're supposed to be thinking about once you're actually on the mound."

"What *are* you supposed to be thinking about?" I asked Gott.

"You're supposed to get somebody out," he said. "That's the only thing you concentrate on. You concentrate on the glove: the catcher's glove. Nothing else. You don't even look at the hitter. But that's hard to teach. My first year in the big leagues I'd see Reggie Jackson and George Brett up there, and I knew it was important to understand that you're just as good as they are and that you can get them out. But all of a sudden a young guy doesn't believe that. That little seed of doubt is planted and the pitcher goes against his game plan. If I'm a power pitcher and Reggie Jackson is a fastball hitter and now suddenly I'm throwing him curve balls, I'm giving in to him. The odds are much better that I can get him out with a fastball, because that's my strength.

"So I see spring training mainly as a time to develop my inner confidence when I'm out there. It's important to work on different types of pitches, different types of situations, work on a little hitch here and there, maybe simplify your mechanics and just keep one or two key checkpoints. That allows you to start the season with all that out of the way, all the cobwebs removed, so that when the bell rings your concentration is purely and solely on getting the batter out. Because the greatest games you ever pitched are the most unconscious efforts—the ones where the rhythm is right and everything flows together.

"Of course, there are always going to be those one or two bad games in a five- or ten-game period when your rhythm is off, so what Ray Miller is teaching us now are things that are going to allow us to kick in when we don't have our good stuff and we're getting battered around a little bit. At those times we can back off and say, 'I've got two key checkpoints, or one checkpoint, and this is how I'm going to do it.'

"One of the things Ray Miller does so well is to teach a principle to somebody and then leave it there. He doesn't dwell on it. He'll let the player think about it, because he knows that when I'm on the mound I'm alone, I'm not with *him*. So I've got to process that as a habit before it works for me in a game. Sometimes I don't get back to him for a couple of weeks or a month. There was one thing Ray talked to me about last year.

As you know, I've been away for a few days, and while I was home I thought more and more about what Ray told me last summer. This morning, as soon as I got back, I went to Ray and I said, 'Do you remember what you told me awhile ago about doing something in my set position?' and he said, 'Yeah,' and I told him, 'I really think that's going to be a good idea.' And he just had a smile on his face and I walked away—but understanding that he had planted the seed, and that he understood that it's going to work when I think it's going to work.''

CHAPTER *17*

Umpires

Just inside the main gate at McKechnie Field, easy to miss because it's so small and nondescript, is a mud-brown building with a sign that says UMPIRES ROOM. Seeing it, I was reminded that umpires also go to spring training, and I wondered whether they also get rusty during the off season and need to work their reflexes back into shape. And what about the rookies—the minor league umpires who get invited to spring training every year to try out for the few openings in the majors?

One day when the Pirates were playing the Phillies, about a half hour before game time, I knocked on the door of the umpires' building and went in. A low partition with a swinging door separated me from the dressing area, where a solidly built man in his early fifties was stripped to his shorts. He had thick black hair, a worldly-wise Mediterranean face and unusually warm brown eyes. He wasn't a man whose authority I would challenge. I asked him if he was a National League umpire, and he said he was—his name was Frank Pulli, and this was his twenty-fifth year in baseball and his seventeenth in the major leagues.

I explained what I wanted to talk to him about. His response was umpire-like: know the facts before you make the call. What kind of book was I writing? Did I have a contract? Who was my publisher? I passed the test, and he indicated a stool where I could sit while he got dressed for the game. None of the other umpires had arrived yet, which was just as well—the umpires' room was no bigger than it had to be.

As we talked, Frank Pulli began to armor himself for the day's work. Without making an inventory, I was aware of a succession of shields and protective pads being strapped on or slipped into place as he slowly got dressed. How many hundreds of times had he performed this ritualized girding of his body for the task of calling balls and strikes? I asked him what spring training means to an umpire.

"You're honing your skills again," he said, "and trying to get in physical shape. The toughest part of this game is the traveling. During the season you're in and out of planes every three days. Most games are at night—by the time you get something to eat, it's time to go to bed, and before you know it it's time to get up. The older you get, the harder it is." Frank Pulli's face was crisscrossed with lines honorably earned in ballparks, airports, buses and hotels. "As an umpire it takes a long time to get up to the majors, but you come down quick.

"Of course it's a mental game too," he said, "and after a while much of it becomes habit. When you're older you can be more relaxed than young umpires who are down here on tryout. Young umpires go all out, which is natural. I remember when *I* was a young umpire in spring training you busted your ass every day trying to get a job."

I asked how umpiring the games of spring compares with umpiring the games of summer. "There's an altogether different atmosphere in spring training," Pulli said. "This is a picnic compared to the regular season. Down here everybody's laid back. The managers are looking at kids, they're not looking at umpires. Besides, they know that the umps are also coming off a five-month layoff. But when the bell rings they'll be screaming."

"Is that relationship as adversarial as ever?"

"No, it's not. Our relationships with players and managers have changed a great deal—for the better—since I came up, mainly because of the big salaries and the long-term contracts. Why would a player come screaming and hollering at you? He's got five more years to play and a million dollars a year. The umpiring is better too."

Two other men arrived and began to change into umpiring garb. Game time was near. Pulli, now fully dressed and presumably fortified against the day's foul balls, went to the door and looked out. A fine rain had begun to fall; in a few minutes he would have to make the first of the afternoon's countless decisions, this one meteorological. He didn't look like a man who was neurotic about making decisions or about what people would think of what he decided.

"I never listen to the hollering after the game," he told me. "I always know that I did the best I could possibly do."

"Why are you in this?" I asked him.

"Because baseball is the greatest game going," he said. "In all the baseball games that have been played, there have never been two alike. I've followed baseball since I was six years old. My dad umpired locally—in the neighborhood of Easton, Pennsylvania—and I used to follow him around."

He started to walk out toward the diamond. The rain was no worse, and the crowd was ready. So was Frank Pulli. This was his third exhibition game of the spring, he told me; he was beginning to feel comfortable with his returning skills.

"Actually," he said, "my first game in spring training is usually my best game in spring training. First of all, you want to show yourself, and then you want to show the players, that you haven't lost it. You're pumped up.

"Once you get it in your blood," he said, "it's very difficult to get it out."

*

The next day the visiting team was the St. Louis Cardinals, and the pregame crowd of codgers and tourists and kids was enjoying watching the National League champions at close range as they took infield practice or ambled over to the railing to sign autographs. Ozzie Smith looked merely human and not superhuman; Whitey Herzog looked avuncular. I decided to drop in again on the umpires' room.

This time three umpires were getting dressed. Two of them conveyed a strong sense of not wanting to talk to a stranger, but the third, a stout and amiable black man in his late thirties, welcomed me warmly. He said that his name was Eric Gregg, that he was from Philadelphia, and that he had been a National League umpire for twelve years.

"This winter I took off fifty pounds," he told me. "There had been a feeling that some of us were too heavy, and I wanted to show people that I'm serious about my condition."

I asked him what he liked about spring training; he was

obviously enjoying being there that afternoon. "Spring training is the best time for umpires," he said. "It's a lot of fun for us. We get to see one another, which we never do during the regular season. I also have my family down here with me. And the games themselves have a more relaxed atmosphere—there's much less pressure.

"This year it's a little different because we've got two new rules—or you might say they're old rules that the league has told us to enforce in 1988. One is the balk rule: the pitcher has to come to a complete stop. That's the kind of rule that you want to call repeatedly in spring training, to make the point before the season starts. The other is the higher strike zone for pitchers—a ball across the letters of the uniform is a *strike*." By his inflection he meant that a ball across the letters has always been a strike in theory but doesn't often get called a strike. Now it really is a strike.

"How long does it take you to get ready for the season?" I asked.

"I need about three good plate jobs to get my eyes ready to call balls and strikes," Gregg said. "On the bases it's not as easy to get ready, because you never know how busy you're going to be. Some days out there you can count your change. Third base can be *really* quiet. But if you miss a checked swing you're up the creek."

"What does it take to be a major league umpire," I asked. "Can it be taught?"

"The main thing you have to have is judgment," he said, "and we can't teach you that. We can teach positioning, and we can teach hustling—getting yourself out to see a play like a trapped ball in the outfield. But we can't teach judgment. Often, judgment is a matter of timing—waiting to let the play happen. Many umpires are too quick. I remember my first major league game. George Foster came up in a critical situation, with runners on base, and the count went to three and two. The next pitch was close, and George checked his swing; he had a very difficult checked swing. I didn't know what to call it. Then George started for the dugout. 'Strike *three!*' I said. He called it for me.

"The thing about spring training," Gregg said, "is that the more you work, the better off you are. If you make a mistake in spring training you want to know *why* you made it. Were you in the wrong position? Did you call it too quick? Because when you know why you made a mistake, then you can correct it."

*

Later in the week I saw Frank Pulli again and I asked him how I could meet one of the tryout umpires. He said one of them was working that day's game. I went into the umpires' room and had no trouble identifying the novice; he had the eagerness to please of all beginners and the reluctance to say much of anything because it might be the wrong thing to say. His name was Ron Barnes, he was from El Cerrito, California, and this was his ninth year in professional baseball; his last year and a half had been spent in the Pacific Coast League. This spring, at the age of twenty-nine, he was one of seven umpires, including the first woman candidate, Pam Postema, competing for two vacancies created by retirement on the National League's twenty-eight-person staff. He had been invited to umpire twenty-five spring training games in order to be evaluated.

"I feel very fortunate to get this exposure," he said, "because I'm trying to make this a career—I'm not just here for fun. My first major league game in spring training was Pittsburgh versus the Texas Rangers. It was very exciting for me." I asked him what differences he had noticed between major league play and what he had seen as an umpire at the lower levels. "In the major leagues the overall play is obviously better," he said. "Plate umpiring is easier, for instance, because the pitching is better—they hit the spots better. But the biggest thing to me is that the players are all a little quicker—they make a hard play look routine—and as a new umpire you have to be conscious of that. But I feel better every day. Every day it's a little more natural."

That afternoon Ron Barnes worked around second base, and I kept an eye on him. Even from a distance he looked young and eager. He was on top of every play, and he made his calls quickly and with gusto; if he was being evaluated from somewhere in the stands, nobody could accuse him of being indecisive. I enjoyed his afternoon. I had the feeling that he was still a few years away but that he would be back.

*

On my last visit to the umpires' room, before a game with the Toronto Blue Jays, the face on the other side of the partition was a remarkably hospitable face. It went with a lopsided smile that said, "You want to talk? Have a seat. How can I help you?"

The name was as American as the face: Bob Davidson. So was the hometown: Des Moines, Iowa. Davidson, who was probably in his late thirties, said he had umpired for eight years in the minors and was now starting his seventh National League season. When I arrived he was sitting on a stool, methodically performing a rite that I had never seen or heard about: taking the shine off the baseballs that would be used that afternoon. On one side he had a bag of five dozen new official National League baseballs, duly certified by the signature of A. Bartlett Giamatti, pres. In front of him on the floor was a tin can filled with a brown substance that looked like axle grease. I asked him what the stuff was.

"It's Delaware River mud," Davidson said. He explained that no other product of man or nature is so uniquely suited to getting the gloss off a new baseball without discoloring it. Because new baseballs are too slippery for a pitcher to fully control, it has long been the duty of the home-plate umpire to give them a rubdown before every major league game.

The procedure calls for an equal application of spit and mud. As we talked, Bob Davidson spat on his hands five dozen times, scooped out a dab of Delaware River mud and rubbed the resulting mixture into the ball. Nothing in his manner suggested that it was a chore or an indignity; they were the motions of a man washing his car or of a cowboy saddling his horse. I said I was surprised that home-plate umpires were stuck with such an inelegant task and couldn't get someone of lesser rank to do it for them. "It's no big deal," Davidson said. "Besides, it's a way to make sure that only the umpire touches the ball before it's put into play." The mud, I later learned, was discovered by Lena Blackburne, a coach of the Philadelphia Athletics, in

Pennsauken Creek, a tributary of the Delaware, in 1938. It has been used every since.

Bob Davidson umpires twelve exhibition games every year in spring training. Getting in physical condition isn't one of his problems—during the fall and winter he referees seventy high school and college basketball games, all over Iowa. "It's more challenging to work a basketball game than to umpire baseball," he said, "because you're in the game more."

In spring training, what's most important to him is to get six or seven games behind the plate. "Umpiring is kind of like riding a bike—once you know how, it comes back," he said. "Still, it takes a little while for calling balls and strikes to come back. Every umpire has a slightly different strike zone. It gets established as your norm after about five years of umpiring, and that's what you want to get back. The first game in spring training is always special. You think, 'Here comes the ball. Wow! There it *is!* It's a lot smaller than a basketball!'

"If they didn't allow us to work spring training it wouldn't be good for us. The players wouldn't like it, either, if you just turned up on opening day."

Working behind the plate is the heart of the profession, Davidson feels. "During the regular season you work there every four days," he says, "and it really tests you. If you're a good base umpire but not a good plate umpire you'll never make it. Behind the plate is our bread and butter."

I asked Bob Davidson what personal qualities the job calls for.

He thought about it for a moment, between spits and rubs. His hands were so dirty that they didn't look as if they would ever get clean.

"What does it take to be an umpire? The ability not to really care what people think. You say, 'That's just baseball.' If you've never been criticized you've never been an umpire. The only way to avoid it is to not show up."

CHAPTER 18

The Toughest Position in Baseball

One day the Pirates went to Kissimmee to play an exhibition game against Houston at the Astros' spring training ballpark. I knew that the whole squad wouldn't make the long bus ride, and I was pretty sure that if I went out to McKechnie Field I'd find the rest of the players being put through a drill. Jim Leyland was the kind of teacher who would never be without a lesson plan.

School was definitely in session when I got to the ballpark, and standing at home plate, hitting fungoes to the outfield, was the only member of the Pirates organization I had previously known as a fan and would have recognized without a score-card: Bill Virdon. Virdon has been part of baseball's landscape for more than thirty years, first as a Cardinal outfielder in 1955, then as a Pirate outfielder from 1956 to 1965, and later as manager of four clubs—the Pirates, Yankees, Astros and Expos—from 1972 to 1984. Now retired from such steady exertions, he works for the Pirates as a special instructor during spring training and also makes four or five trips with their minor league teams during the summer.

Seeing him there in the Florida sun, I thought of how many clubs bring back one or two of their former stars every spring—often giants like Ted Williams, Stan Musial, Al Kaline and Sandy Koufax—to be teachers in residence. Aging gracefully, familiar gods in a sea of unfamiliar faces, they are ornaments of spring training. Nobody else so embodies the continuity of the game or so strongly tugs on the memories of the codgers in the stands.

I recognized Bill Virdon because nobody in baseball looks quite like him. Now fifty-eight and gray-haired, he is still a slender and scholarly figure who gives the impression—partly because of his distinctive metal-rimmed glasses—of having strayed into the ballpark while trying to find the library. Scholarship, however, takes many forms, and as Virdon wielded the fungo bat with casual ease, stroking fly after fly to the farthest outfielders, I thought of how many tens of thousands of practice balls he has hit in his long career of teaching the game's fundamentals. The fungo bat was as much a part of his uniform as his cap—the badge of his craft. No ode has been written to that elongated piece of wood, and even the *American Heritage Dictionary* doesn't know how it got its name, but where would spring training be without it?

When Virdon's drill was over, I introduced myself and told him I had long admired his integrity as both a player and a manager—he seemed to be one of those strong, silent Midwestern types who exemplify the best values of the game. I found myself looking into a pair of direct blue eyes behind the metal-rimmed glasses.

"I think spring training is a necessity to keep the game on a level that we like for it," Virdon told me. "One reason is that so many players come up today after only a year or two in the minors. Another big difference from when I started playing is that there are twenty-six major league clubs instead of sixteen, so the talent is spread out more, and we have to get the maximum out of the players we've got. We have to teach them more and stay after them, because there isn't some other guy standing behind them. When I was playing, if we didn't produce, somebody was right there to take our spot."

Virdon's main responsibility in the Pirates camp was to work with the outfielders. "I think outfield play is one of the neglected areas in the business," he said, "though not as much as it used to be. My job is to make sure the players get the work they need on handling the ball in different situations and other fundamentals that are necessary to play the outfield and play it well, because that's the way you win baseball games. It can't all be taught with a fungo bat and by exposure to another outfielder. It takes a certain amount of playing time to know what kind of situations come up. You have to know your runners, and who's hitting, and things like that."

Again, there was no escaping "the fundamentals." What are the fundamentals of outfield play, I asked Virdon, and how does he teach them?

"The thing that comes to mind immediately when you ask about fundamentals," he said, "is where to throw the ball. If you're throwing to a relay man you want to throw high, for the simple reason that the relay man has to catch your throw and make the play back toward the infield. If you throw the ball low, he's got to go away from the infield to meet it and catch it. That takes all his momentum away; he has to bend down and then straighten up and turn around and throw."

Virdon demonstrated how many seconds this ungainly motion would consume. "But if you throw high, the infielder can turn toward the infield as part of the same motion and go right on in with his throw. Also, you always have a 'trailer' on relays—that's a backup guy—so if you miss the first guy, you want to miss him high so that the second guy can make the play.

"The other important play is throwing to the bases—throwing to third, for instance, or throwing home. There you have to emphasize that the throw must be *low*—and not just because it's easier to make the tag. You also want the throw to be low so that somebody in the infield can handle it if the throw is off; or if the throw is too late to get *this* runner, you can keep the other runner from taking an extra base."

Virdon stopped to sign an autograph for a retired couple who had ambled onto the field; security in spring training is somewhat laissez-faire. "What's your name?" the husband asked. Virdon told him. "My name's Bill too," the old man said. It was obvious that he had never heard of Bill Virdon. Virdon took this with Missouri equanimity. The man began a leisurely explanation of how he and his wife were just driving around Florida, taking in the sights. This morning they had come over the bridge from St. Petersburg, and as long as they were in Bradenton anyway. . . . Finally Virdon said, "Now I have to ask something of you. I have to ask you to go back behind that railing." The old couple said goodbye and left.

"Those two throws I was telling you about," Virdon said, resuming his account, "are throws that I think are vital and that are abused a great deal. The reason they're abused is that playing the outfield is a situation where you don't get to do it much. If you don't really think about it and work on it in practice, you develop all kinds of bad tendencies—you're rushing and you try to throw the ball too hard, and it flies out and gets away from you. So it takes some attention and some *thought* to play the outfield. Basically, outfielders have to *think* what they have to do with the ball when they come up with it, and if you as the coach don't stay with them it slips away. It's not intentional, but it's something that has to be worked on constantly.

"Unfortunately, baseball is hard to practice under game conditions. In practice you never get the adrenaline going and you're never in the same situation that you are in a game. In a game, the run that's scored might be the big run. But in practice you're never working at that level of competition, so you're a little bit cautious. Then when it happens in a game you rush, and things go wrong. It's like hitting—you never hit in batting practice the way you do in a game, because the competition's not as good. Some hitters can keep that level up in practice and some can't."

Of all the outfielding fundamentals, none is as fundamental as catching a fly ball. I wondered how Virdon taught that skill.

"There's only one way of working at it," he said. "The outfielder has to catch a tremendous number of fly balls off the fungo. I strongly believe that there's a way for an outfielder to work off a fungo. I don't know if I can explain it, but the point is that the player must keep away from anticipation. If you're an outfielder you've got to make sure you see the ball and let your eyes do your work for you. I don't want outfielders to respond on the basis of how I swing my bat; I want to make sure they see the ball before they break after it. For example, many times when I'm trying to hit the ball over their head I'll pop it up in front of them instead. If they've started to go back on the basis of how hard I swung they're in trouble. During my own playing days, that's when I felt I was really getting something out of working off the fungo. I'd be working on balls hit over my head, but I was ready for anything that was hit. But that's really hard to do in practice. As a coach you have to keep after them and keep after them and keep after them, and they have to keep working and keep working and keep working on handling the ball and transferring it. It's just a matter of labor."

Though Virdon seemed to be as far away from his pupils as a teacher can get—he at home plate with a fungo, they three hundred feet off with a glove—he said he spends much of his time with them in the outfield, seeing that they execute properly and make the right throwing decisions, especially on cutoff and relay plays in drills that involve the whole team.

"At that point," Virdon said, "all I do, usually, if they throw to the wrong base or if they throw a ball too high or too low— whatever I'm trying to teach—is to get on them a little bit. I don't tell them in advance where to throw the ball, because that's an instinct play, and they've got to develop those instincts themselves. For example, if you've got a fast runner on first and the ball's not hit hard, you should know in your own mind whether you've got a chance to get him at third or not. If he's a slow runner he probably won't go. But that's judgment: it's a matter of where the ball is hit, how hard it's hit and who the runner is.

"Of course, we practice the cutoff play a great deal—it's one of the most important plays in baseball. Let's say you're trying to throw out a runner going from first to third on a single, but your throw isn't going to get him, so someone in the infield cuts it off. That's for the simple reason that the guy who hit the ball is usually just as important as the guy you're trying to throw out at third, because if he gets to second he can score on a single, whereas if you keep him at first you've got a chance for a double play. Also, it generally takes two hits, not one, to score him from first."

I wondered whether it affected the play of an outfielder to be in such a lonely occupation, far from the central drama of the game. I remembered a time, not all that long ago, when the crowd at Yankee Stadium was allowed to walk across the field after the game to reach the subway stairs just beyond the bleachers. I always stopped in center field and looked back; home plate was a mile away. In my imagination I was Joe DiMaggio, loping effortlessly across that vast expanse to snare tremendous drives that no other mortal would have caught up with. And yet . . . wouldn't it be possible, even for DiMaggio, even for *me*, to let the attention slip amid such solitude—to daydream, to think about something else, to fail to see the ball as it came off the distant bat?

"I think the outfield is the toughest position in baseball to play—for just that reason," Virdon said. "In the course of a ball game you've got 120 or 130 pitches, and an outfielder on a busy day will have seven or eight plays. It's next to impossible to keep an outfielder mentally alert on 130 pitches. You can keep telling them and keep telling them, but if they don't learn to do it they will always have trouble playing the outfield."

R. J. Reynolds came in from right field, and I asked him how he handles the isolation. "It gets lonely out there, no doubt about it," he said. "You have to keep your intensity level. But it's like anything else—if you know who you're playing with, you become a unit. You talk a lot. For instance, I'm in right field, so I've got the bullpen, and sometimes I talk to those guys. But mostly I've got Andy Van Slyke. He's pretty interesting. He keeps himself loose—hollering or whatever he wants to do—and he entertains me with that stuff. Sometimes he's a commentator out there, so that makes it fun.''

Patience is said to come with age, despite frequent evidence to the contrary, and the Pirates were very young. I asked Virdon whether he found it harder to get kids to pay attention in the outfield than older players.

"I think it might be the other way around," he said. "Youngsters are so eager to make it in the big leagues that they'll basically do what you're trying to get them to do. Older players today have a lot of other things on their mind. You put them out in the outfield and they start to think about what happened yesterday and what'll happen tomorrow—and bingo! The ball's hit to them and they're not ready." I wondered whether those "other things" were such things as money and contracts and agents and owners—all the new financial and legal baggage that modern ballplayers find themselves toting.

"Not necessarily," Virdon said. "It could be anything. The older you get, the more you've got going on. It could be family, it could be a problem with your wife, it could be your kids, it could be any number of things. It's all a matter of self-discipline. As a coach you try to instill it, and the good outfielders learn to do it. The guys who fall by the wayside never do. Sometimes even the good players aren't able to do it all the time. But the best ones are total in their self-discipline."

*

As the end of spring training approached, I remembered that Bill Virdon, unlike the other Pirates, would now be putting his uniform away. His hardest work of the season—six intensive weeks—was ending and he would be going back home to Springfield, Missouri. I asked him why he continues to come to spring training.

"To get out of the cold," he said.

He could see that I expected a better answer.

"Because I work with a good staff," he said.

I continued to look at him.

"To stay in touch with the game," he said.

CHAPTER 19

Play Ball!

There's no question about when spring training ends: it ends on opening day. Abruptly, the weeks of preparation merge into the months of reality. Hopes and dreams are no longer good enough; when a game is lost it gets added to the loss column, that dismal daily barometer of missed chances and failed aspirations.

The Pirates' home opener was a night game with the Phillies, and I went out to attend the rites that would conclude my book. I flew to Pittsburgh in the early afternoon and bought a copy of the *Pittsburgh Post-Gazette* at the airport. BUCS SELL OUT HOME OPENER, said a headline at the top of page one, and the accompanying story began: "For the first time since they moved into Three Rivers Stadium in 1970 the Pirates are asking people not to come to the ballpark. Tonight's home opener is the first advance sellout ever for the Pirates and will be the largest baseball crowd ever in Pittsburgh—58,727."

I thought of how small the crowds had been at Three Rivers Stadium during the first season and a half of the Thrift-Leyland regime, before the turnaround began, and one story in particular came back to me. The Dodgers were in town, and their manager, Tommy Lasorda, told Jim Leyland, "I see more people than this at a restaurant in Los Angeles."

Sellout fever was in the air as I walked across the yellow steel bridge to the stadium at five o'clock. Game time was two hours away, but the parking lot was already half filled with Pirate fans who had come from all over the tristate area by car, van, pickup truck, school bus and chartered bus. Quite a few were college students—I saw Trailways buses with signs that said Slippery Rock University, Grove City College and Indiana University of Pennsylvania. Food was also in the air: the smoky smell of barbecue and shish kebab, emanating from charter bus groups that had brought cooking tents and stoves. Many families had brought tailgate picnics. It was like no baseball crowd I had seen in New York; there the point is to scramble out of the subway and into the ballpark. This was like a football crowd: husbands and wives and children and teenagers enjoying themselves and each other. The game could wait. Let somebody else watch infield practice.

It was a perfect spring afternoon, and it began to turn into a perfect spring evening. People walking from the city's "Golden Triangle" swarmed across the bridge; party boats on the Allegheny River tooted their horns; a full moon came up over the postmodern towers of the new Pittsburgh. For one night, at least, all the signs of civic recovery were in place. Jim Leyland had said that a team that hustled would win its fans back. His young Pirates had hustled and the crowd was here. Now they had to do something harder. They had to win.

I had asked Syd Thrift if I could sit with him during the

game, and the time had come to look for him. I entered Three Rivers Stadium at the press gate and found myself in a long tunnel. Underfoot it had green carpeting of the kind that leads out to the swimming pool in second-rate motels. I followed the carpet and it led me into the Pirates' dugout and in turn—at the same level—out onto the field. This was Astroturf? I had always thought Astroturf was artificial grass, somewhat resembling a doormat. I never knew that when sportscasters talked about "the rug" they were actually talking about a rug.

For a minute I thought I had blundered into the wrong tunnel. But then I saw the Pirates taking infield practice and Gene Lamont hitting fungoes to the outfielders; they were really playing baseball on this stuff. It was an unusually depressing moment—the texture of the game had vanished from under my feet. I stood on the carpet next to the dugout and gazed up at the circular stadium. I was in an immense dungeon, three tiers high and totally enclosed. There was no glimpse of scenery or skyline or neighborhood anywhere to tell me that the stadium was in Pittsburgh. We could have been in Palermo or Pyongyang.

I saw Thrift standing near first base, talking to a reporter and spitting on the carpet. At least one of the verities was intact. Thrift took me up to his private box. He was wearing a dark blue suit and looking like a proper general manager. A Pirates directors' meeting had been held that afternoon, Thrift explained, and he had used the occasion to tell the board about the four-seam fastball.

"I could see the bewilderment in their eyes," he said. "I told them I wanted them to be the first board of directors in the history of baseball to hear about the aerodynamics of the game.

I wanted them to know that we're the most advanced club in baseball in technology. Jim Gott throws 95 miles per hour with a four-seam fastball and 91 miles per hour with a two-seam fastball, and I want them to understand that."

From Thrift's box I looked around the huge stadium. The only advertisements I could see were corporate and discreet: Gulf Oil, Heinz, Westinghouse, Mellon Bank, PPG Industries, USX, Pittsburgh National Bank, Equibank, Dravo, US Air. I thought of the amiable billboards I had grown up with in the Polo Grounds, promoting the simpler products of a simpler age: Adam Hats, Breyer's Ice Cream, Gem Blades, GGG Suits, Muriel Cigars, Mrs. Wagner's Pies. Where is Mrs. Wagner today, and who wears an Adam hat? Or any hat?

The public address system called us to order. "Welcome to another exciting season of Pirate baseball!" said a rotund voice. It was seven o'clock, and every seat appeared to be filled. Around second base a phalanx of girls arrived, carrying clusters of big balloons, and in center field a marching band materialized. "And now, ladies and gentlemen," said the announcer, "here . . . are . . . your . . . 1988 . . . Pittsburgh . . . Pirates!" The 1988 Pittsburgh Pirates were individually introduced, including the two trainers, the equipment manager, and the strength and conditioning coach, Dr. Warren Sipp, and they trotted out and stood along the first-base line. The manager was the last to be called—"Now in his third season, Jim Leyland!"—and got the biggest hand. Seen from aloft, the Pirates were tiny figures: uniformed athletes on a distant stage. The boys of Bradenton had been packed away for another year.

Bishop Donald Wuerl of the Pittsburgh Catholic

Archdiocese delivered the invocation, asking God, among other things, "to look on this team with a warm smile." He also asked God "to smile on the visiting team"—a request that drew scattered boos for the assembled Phillies—"and on every team that comes to this stadium." Turning to temporal concerns, Bishop Wuerl concluded with a prayer for "not too many unearned runs during the season."

The national anthem would be sung, the announcer said, by "Mr. Lee Greenwood, winner of four gold albums," and it was. When Mr. Greenwood released "the land of the free-ee-ee" into the night air of Pittsburgh, the girls in the infield released their hundreds of colored balloons, which floated up and out of the cavernous stadium. The atmosphere was festive, World Series–like. To throw out the first ball, Fred Rogers was summoned to the mound. "On the twentieth anniversary of Public Television's longest-running children's show," the announcer said, "Pittsburgh is proud that *Mister Rogers' Neighborhood* began right here!" Rogers made a terrible pitch into the dirt. Mike LaValliere blocked it and brought it back to Rogers. "Mike's been blocking pitches like that for a week," Thrift said—an allusion to the fact that in the Pirates' final games of spring training, certain pitchers' split-fingered fastballs hadn't reached optimum refinement.

"Play ball!" said umpire Gerry Davis. Juan Samuel stepped to the plate. Doug Drabek got the sign from LaValliere, peered at Samuel, and pitched. Spring training was over.

*

Samuel popped up to José Lind at second. That was good. Milt Thompson singled. That was bad.

Thompson tried to steal and LaValliere threw him out. That was good. Phil Bradley reached on an error at third. That was bad. Mike Schmidt grounded out to end the inning. No problem.

Barry Bonds, leading off for the Pirates against Kevin Gross, got a cheer from the crowd and hit a triple off the wall. Lind struck out. Andy Van Slyke tripled to score Bonds. Two triples! Impressive. Bobby Bonilla struck out and Sid Bream came up. Thrift commented on Bream's new stance—the one Bream had told me he was working to establish in spring training. Bream stroked a ball that was caught at the 400-foot sign in deepest center field. Pirates 1–0.

Neither team scored in the second inning, but Bonds opened the third with a home run. Pirates 2–0.

Phil Bradley led off the fourth for the Phillies. "This guy's always in for the averages—he's a pretty productive hitter," Thrift said as Bradley stepped up. Bradley promptly singled, and Mike Schmidt brought him home with a double over third. Pirates 2–1.

Nobody scored in the fifth. Somebody asked Thrift about the Phillies' right fielder, Chris James. "I like him," Thrift said, and he mentioned some of James's strengths. He was as studious of the Phillies' players as he was of his own. I asked him whether he traveled with the Pirates when they play on the road. He said that he did and that he also tries to catch a high school game in the afternoon. I only spoke to him between innings; during the game he was mostly silent, hard at work at what he does best—watching ballplayers.

Defensively, the Pirates were executing well. In the third, Bream started a graceful double play, throwing to shortstop Al

Pedrique at second, who threw back to Drabek at first, and in the fifth inning R. J. Reynolds, LaValliere and Pedrique collaborated on a relay—right fielder to catcher to shortstop—that nailed Samuel at second base and stifled a Phillies rally. They were just the kind of plays I had seen the Pirates endlessly practicing in spring training under Bill Virdon and Tommy Sandt.

The sixth inning brought the game's emotional climax. Bradley, Schmidt and Von Hayes singled off Drabek, filling the bases with nobody out. Leyland relieved Drabek and brought in Vincente Palacios, the rookie right hander I had last seen in the clubhouse at Bradenton, when his minimal English and my minimal Spanish turned out to have no overlapping words. I was surprised that Leyland called on the kid from Mexico to pitch with the bases full in a game of such psychic importance to so many fans. (Official attendance had just been announced at 54,098, a new Pirate record.) I mentioned this to Thrift and he half agreed ("There aren't this many people in Mexico"), but he added: "The kid is foxy."

Palacios was as foxy as a burglar. Normally a power pitcher, he set up the batters with change-ups that caught the corners of the plate, and then came in with his fastball. Thrift was enjoying the kid's nerve. The fans were enjoying it less; their new season was on the line, and they were quiet and edgy. Palacios didn't keep them waiting: Lance Parrish popped up to Bream, Chris James fouled out to LaValliere, and Steve Jeltz flied out to Bonds. The fans stood up and went crazy. "That inning gives them something to talk about," Thrift said.

In the seventh and eighth, Palacios was no less foxy, striking out three and giving up just one single. But the game was still too close; the crowd wanted an insurance run. In the bottom of the eighth, Bonilla walked with two out, Bream doubled, and Reynolds was walked to fill the bases. LaValliere, up next, took two strikes; the luxury of an insurance run faded. Then he crashed a double, high off the right-field wall, scoring three. Jubilation.

Jeff Robinson came in to work the ninth, shutting down the Phillies with his split-fingered fastball. I asked Thrift why Palacios had been taken out. "You take him out so nothing will go bad," he said. "He'll have that good experience to remember next time he pitches." The remark took me back one last time to spring training. I remembered Ray Miller, an incurable optimist in a negative game, forcing the power of positive thinking on his pitchers. Tonight Palacios had been positive he could get the Phillies out.

*

But the man whose achievement lingered with me was Syd Thrift. In just two years he had conjured out of nowhere this born-again Pittsburgh crowd and this born-again club of young players who already looked as if they could make a respectable run for the pennant. Thrift was a bundle of paradoxes. His feet were planted in the soil of rural America and his head was in the clouds of high technology. He chewed Red Man tobacco and quoted Igor Sikorsky on the aerodynamics of a baseball in flight. He was a pragmatist and a visionary. He worshiped education and talked like a gospel preacher. Not since Branch Rickey, it seemed to me, had such a piquant mixture of traits turned up in baseball's operating machinery, and I asked Thrift whether he had had any model in mind when he became Pittsburgh's general manager.

He shook his head. He said that the idea of a model for the general manager's job had never occurred to him. But the question seemed to nag at him, and he didn't say anything more as we made our way out of Three Rivers Stadium, joining the crowd heading toward the parking lot. It was a happy crowd, in no hurry to get home.

Finally Thrift said, "I once had a very vivid dream. It was just when I was about to leave the Royals Baseball Academy, back in 1971. I felt like I had learned so much while I was running the academy, and I was so excited every day. I had seen breakthroughs in so many areas—baserunning, and baseballs in flight, and on and on and on. And at the same time I knew that the Royals organization wasn't the least bit interested in what we were doing. They were trying to say, 'It ain't so.' Cedric Tallis and Lou Gorman didn't want to hear or believe anything. They didn't even think Frank White was a prospect. It was an uphill battle, and after a while you get tired of running uphill. So I was rassling every day: 'Are we really doing all the great things I see us doing?' Because I hear that we ain't doing it. That we're throwing away all this money. Which seems like nothing today, as you look back on it."

Thrift's voice had an edge of anger that I hadn't heard before.

"I never knew Branch Rickey," Thrift went on, "but I admired him. I knew all the contributions he had made, because I had been around a number of his disciples—men like Clyde Sukeforth and Rex Bowen—and I had heard stories every day about his theories and his philosophies and about how innova-

tive he had been in the training and development and measure-
ment of players. But in my own work in those same areas I
was getting no support from my organization. You need that
support. It was a hard time for me.

"Then one night I had this dream. It was crystal clear to me
that Branch Rickey and Mrs. Rickey came down to Florida to
see the Baseball Academy. And as they went around that
complex with me Mr. Rickey kept saying, 'Marvelous!' 'What
a great idea!' 'What great thinking!' 'Oh, this is wonderful!'
And he asked me all kinds of questions—how were we doing
this and what had we learned about that?—and Mrs. Rickey
was right there with him, and we were all riding in a golf cart.
I don't know how we all got in that golf cart, but we managed.
And Mrs. Rickey thought it was such a marvelous thing, too,
because Mr. Rickey thought it was such a marvelous thing. I
had never seen the woman in my life, but she was just as clear
as could be. I can picture her to this day.

"When I woke up the next morning I felt as if that was the
greatest thing that ever happened to me, because Mr. Rickey
had endorsed what I was doing. And yet he was dead; he wasn't
on this earth. Isn't that amazing? But what he said was crystal
clear. He said, 'You're twenty-five to fifty years ahead of your
time.' That's exactly what he said. 'And you're going to have
to learn to bear with that,' he said, 'because when you're ahead
of your time you're going to get a lot of criticism. But the fact
is that you're ahead of your time and these are great ideas.'
And I said, 'Well, what a compliment!' "

Epilogue

The momentum of spring training carried into the season: the Pirates got off to their best start since 1937, setting a club record for wins in April. They were in first place or tied for first place from April 13 to May 2. Overtaken by the Mets, they dropped to second place and stayed there for the rest of the season except for four days—one in July and three in August—when they were dislodged by the Expos. In mid-July they won 12 out of 13 games and pulled to within a half-game of the Mets on July 21. A month later, on August 21, they were still only 3½ games out, and they remained serious contenders until the first week of September, when they fell to 10 games behind. A late slump, combined with the Mets' closing spurt, widened the final gap to 15 games, but the won-and-lost record (85 and 75) was the Pirates' best since 1979 and their second-place finish was well ahead of the Expos, Cubs, Cardinals and Phillies. "The Mets are the best team—that's what we learned this season," Jim Leyland said. "We didn't win, not because we were too young but because we weren't quite good enough." Andy Van Slyke was the club's conspicuous star, a runner-up for Most Valuable Player of the year in the National League. Van Slyke and Bobby Bonilla both had 100 runs batted in; Doug Drabek's 15–7 led the pitchers, and Jim Gott's 34 saves were the second-highest in the league. Attendance was exceptional from the beginning. The previous year's mark was passed on July 23, and the total attendance of 1,865,713, an average of 23,321 per game, broke the all-time Pirate record of 1,705,828, set in Forbes Field in 1960. By every standard the season far surpassed the expectations for the club in Syd Thrift's third year.

Three days after the season ended, Thrift was fired. The vote of the Pirates' sixteen-member board was unanimous, with one abstention—that of the mayor of Pittsburgh, Sophie Masloff. The board's president, Carl F. Barger, had assumed that position in the fall of 1987 when Thrift forced the ouster of "Mac" Prine in a fight over final authority in baseball decisions.

Round Two of the fight was played out in the summer of 1988. Newspaper accounts of Thrift's dismissal suggest what happened. The Associated Press said, "Thrift's acknowledged egotism, his inability to work closely with Pirates president Carl Barger and board chairman Douglas Danforth, and his reluctance to share the credit for the Pirates' resurgence wore thin with the board, composed mostly of corporate executives." Joe L. Brown, Thrift's original patron, said, "There were a number of times when he [Thrift] appeared to have a lack of understanding of the requisite business relationship that when you work for someone, they're the boss." President Barger summed it up: "Syd had a perception of what his authority should be and we had a different perception."

Pitcher Jim Gott, quoted in an adjacent column of the *Pittsburgh Post-Gazette*, said: "I believe in the guy. I'm really sorry he's leaving. He's the James Dean of baseball. He was a rebel. He had a lot of new ideas. He wanted to bring new things into baseball, and his new ideas helped the players be as armed as they could be."

Syd Thrift told the *Post-Gazette:* "I feel good about the job I did. It wasn't perfect, but when you analyze where we came from, where we are and where we're going, I have to feel good—not for me but for the franchise. I have inner peace. Very few people have that. I have peace beyond all understanding. I really do. My wife Dolly was crying—and that's tough for her after being married to me for thirty-two years—and I said, 'Stop crying now. These have been the three greatest years of my life, so stop crying and be thankful.' "

Acknowledgments

For various gifts freely offered I want to thank

- David Wolff, the editor who asked me if I had ever thought of writing a baseball book

- Dan Denton, the friend who grew up in Bradenton and who steered me to unusually helpful people there

- Howard Hall, columnist of the *Bradenton Herald*, who was particularly generous with his hospitality and knowledge

- Barbara Damstra, librarian of the *Bradenton Herald*, who found whatever I was looking for

- Kent Chetlain and Arthur C. Schofield, who were willing providers of local history and information

- Mary Roush Allen, who opened the door to Edd Roush— and much more

- Jim Leyland, his coaches and his players, who were unfailingly open and forthcoming to a stranger in their midst

- Rick Cerrone and Greg Johnson of the Pittsburgh Pirates organization, who gave permission and let me in

- Charles P. Willis, my boyhood friend and fellow baseball addict, now a Pittsburgher and a helpful scout
- Stephanie Vardavas, for good counsel, as always
- John S. Rosenberg, once again, for his sensitive editing and valuable editorial guidance on the manuscript

Sources

The Baseball Encyclopedia: The Complete and Official Record of Major League Baseball, Joseph L. Reichler, ed. 6th ed. (New York: Macmillan, 1985). This astonishing 2,733-page volume was my best friend. I kept it within reach at all times and never ceased to marvel at its thoroughness.

"A History of Spring Training in Florida and Bradenton," an address given to the Manatee County Historical Society, February 18, 1970, by Jabbo Gordon. My chapter "Florida Days" is indebted to this amiable talk, which I found in the excellent Manatee County Library in Bradenton.

The Glory of Their Times: The Story of the Early Days of Baseball Told by the Men Who Played It, by Lawrence S. Ritter (New York: Macmillan, 1966). The incident recalled by Paul Waner that I've quoted in Chapter 7 is typical of the rich detail in this engaging book. Edd Roush, incidentally, was one of the twenty-two old-timers who told their stories to Ritter.

Yesterday's Bradenton, by Arthur C. Schofield (Lindsay Curtis Publishing Company, 1984). A pleasant local history, full of old photographs.

The Baseball Fan's Guide to Spring Training, by Mike Shatzkin and Jim Charlton (Reading, Mass.: Addison-Wesley, 1988). The dope on every spring training park in Florida and Arizona—an enjoyable mixture of tourist information, baseball history and statistical lore.

The Baseball Hall of Fame library, Cooperstown, N.Y. The librarians at this great archive answered my most obscure questions with good cheer, unsurprised that someone would want to know, for instance, who discovered Delaware River mud as the ideal baseball rubdown.

Index of Baseball
Names